LAW AND FREEDOM IN
THE SCHOOL

THE UNIVERSITY OF CHICAGO PRESS
CHICAGO, ILLINOIS

THE BAKER AND TAYLOR COMPANY
NEW YORK

THE CAMBRIDGE UNIVERSITY PRESS
LONDON

THE MARUZEN-KABUSHIKI-KAISHA
TOKYO, OSAKA, KYOTO, FUKUOKA, SENDAI

THE MISSION BOOK COMPANY
SHANGHAI

LAW AND FREEDOM
IN THE SCHOOL

"Can and Cannot," "Must and Must Not,"
"Ought and Ought Not" in Pupils' Projects

By
GEORGE A. COE
Teachers College, Columbia University

THE UNIVERSITY OF CHICAGO PRESS
CHICAGO ILLINOIS

Composed and Printed By
The University of Chicago Press
Chicago, Illinois, U.S.A.

PREFACE

The theme of this essay is law as a factor in school projects—natural law (the "cans and cannots"), common and statute law (the "musts and must nots"), and moral law (the "oughts and ought nots"). Many pens have discoursed of late upon the educative possibilities that reside in the pupil's own will when it freely develops in an appropriate social environment; let me speak of that within or roundabout every project that conditions his will.

Law, then, not merely or chiefly as subject-matter to be studied, but as a dynamic factor in project-situations, and as an actual or possible control therein—this is the field of our study. Purposeful activity on the part of the pupil is the most educative experience in the world, no doubt; but what starts purposes going, what gives them their content, how much of the actual purpose comes to clear definition, and how much is wrought of which neither teacher nor pupil takes account? Again, since the school is a purposeful activity of society, pupils' projects must be thought of as being, at the same time, projects of the larger, encompassing will. What, then, is the actual relation, and what the desirable relation, between these two factors in school experience?

So inveterate is the habit of assuming that free purposes, at least in the case of children, are antithetical to law, that to bring law into the foreground, as I am about to do, may seem to imply rejection, distrust, or an

v

intended restriction of the project method. But this
would be a misunderstanding. In order that my readers
may not mistake any of the points that I am driving at,
let me say abruptly and bluntly that I am writing this
essay under a conviction that the project method has
come into education—has been coming into it for more
than a century—to stay there, and to grow until it
dominates schools of all grades. It is not a tool that our
taste or convenience picks out from several alternatives,
but primarily a law of mind and character; therefore,
not something to be selected or rejected, trusted or dis-
trusted, restricted or extended, but understood and incorporated into our purposes as teachers just as we incorporate plant physiology into agriculture.

I am using the term project, of course, in the sense
that makes purposing, and particularly purposing
together, its distinctive mark. Not the material worked
upon, nor the products that result; not action with
accompanying satisfaction; not pleased attention, but
purposeful self-guidance. This connotes desire; conflict
between desires; selection through discriminating judgment; forethought and planning; fitting means to ends;
carrying a planned activity through; judging the product
and one's self by means of it, and thus making ready for
further self-guided action. Purposing, in this full sense
and range, is nothing less than the process—and it
alone contains the generative force—whereby one
comes to one's self as a person. Used collectively, it
is the democratic process. Our theme represents,
therefore, a part of the general problem of how democracy can come into existence, and how it can improve
itself.

On the other hand, I am sure that we have only begun to comprehend the educative project. Some factors in it are obscure and even elusive; the relative isolation of the school from what is called "the world's work" conceals various factors; some factors, as I shall show, actually produce illusory interpretations of experience. What I hope to do, then, is to bring such facts to light in order that a fuller and more effective use of the principle may be made. If, for a time, limitations of the project as it is commonly conceived are made much of, and if barriers to the use of it seem to be in process of erection, in the end the project-approach will be shown to be capable of solving its own difficulties. The principle will exhibit its vitality, not by proving that it can tolerate exceptions, not by going around obstacles, but by going through them in the strength of its inherent truth and value.

GEORGE A. COE

THE GLENDORA FOOTHILLS SCHOOL
GLENDORA, CALIFORNIA
March, 1923

TABLE OF CONTENTS

CHAPTER I

THE DEPENDENCE OF PROJECTS
UPON LAW

That the best-laid plans of mice and men depend for their outcome upon something else than planning; that law besets us behind and before; that our freedom, though it be worth all the world to us, is at most but a pearl within an ocean; yes, that our freedom is achieved only in and through obedience to law—all this is a commonplace comment upon life. We hear it over and over. That it holds for school projects, and must needs be one determinant of what we are to mean by project method, should require no argument.

Yet, in our eagerness to free the teacher and the pupil from hampering, largely artificial, laws imposed by the school of yesterday, we thus far in the project movement have been interested in freedom and the consequences thereof rather than in the conditions and the limitations of freedom.

Therefore, it may be worth while to contemplate pupils' projects from this neglected angle. In the present chapter an endeavor will be made to bring to clear consciousness what we ordinarily overlook. We shall for the most part pass in review teaching situations and processes of familiar types, merely noting factors that, in subsequent chapters, will be subjected to analysis in order to ascertain the bearing that such facts have upon the whole theory of the project.

Probably no type of project received so early, distinguished, and nearly unanimous approval by eminent educators as college athletics. Here we have initiative on the part of students; team work; self-imposed discipline; management that requires continuity and perseverance; consequences that count, and student judgment upon achievement. Who has not heard college presidents speak glowingly of the educational values of this experience, particularly of the development of rigid self-control on the part of individuals, and of training in social unity and co-operation? But some consequences occurred that were not "denominated in the bond." What happened when the football team "broke training" for good at the end of the season was not in the educational spotlight; only rarely did the sort of business training acquired in competitive, gate-receipt games come before the footlights; none but a few inquisitive scientific minds stopped to find out what physiological after-effects might be expected. "I cannot dive in my old form," said a "grad" to me when we were swimming together some five years after he had finished his football career; "I supposed that I was through with my knee injury when I left the university, but I find that I was not."

A single glance like this at unplanned-for by-products of students' projects in athletics should be sufficient to remind us that ordinary natural laws, physiological and psychological, grind out results, good and bad, on their own account—that is, without regard to the good intentions of the students or of their faculty advisers.

A boy who had conceived the project of making a hammock spent a considerable amount of his Saturday time sawing and whittling out the necessary "needle." When his labor seemed about to be rewarded by the possession of a tool ready for use, the frail timber that he had chosen to work with split, and the whole project, for the time at least, was frustrated. Very likely this experience was more valuable for this boy than easy success would have been, but in any case what happened to him educationally was determined not merely by the fact that he purposed something and proceeded to execute it, but in part by conditioning natural-law factors that did their work entirely apart from his purpose.

The obverse of this case may be seen in children whose projects, though well defined as to the product desired and as to the material to be wrought, turn awry because muscular strength, or muscular co-ordination, or mental continuity, is insufficient for the task. Any one or more of several consequences may ensue, as the breaking-up of a co-operating group because one member cannot do his share, yet insists upon doing something; discouragement of initiative; a habit of self-depreciation or of fretting; "faking." One is justified in wondering what really happens, educationally, by reason of the unfinished jobs that strew the path of such organizations as Boy Scouts. "Yes, I know how to do it," said one of them to me. "Show me, then," said I. It turned out that his project of acquiring one of the Scout skills had been carried through in his imagination only. Doubtless, under some conditions the experience of failure can be highly educative, but the conditions need to be carefully scrutinized. Again, many projects require a succession of decisions, of which the first is likely to be the easiest. Suppose a pupil is simply incapable of sustaining his

interest in the face of increasing and unforeseen difficulties. He has started, he is willing to do his part,
but nature prevents him from going on, and the educative results are determined partly by this fact.

Some city boys start to make "pushmobiles" for
themselves out of grocers' boxes and old roller skates.
Here, one would say, is a project that may be made
educationally valuable. But the teacher happens to
know that the "pushmobile," by exercising the two legs
unequally and unsymmetrically, produces deformities.[1]
The teacher's experience proves, too, the practical impos-
sibility of inducing children systematically to change
sides with this plaything so as to exercise both legs alike.
Therefore, the making of "pushmobiles" in the school
shop is not permitted.   For the moment let us postpone
the question how a teacher might best handle a situation
like this; let us simply contemplate the fact that the
future welfare of the child, as determined by natural
laws, becomes through the teacher a "Thou shalt not,"
which no urgency of the pupil's purpose can revoke.
Perhaps all children aspire to grow up and be strong,
but the conditions of doing so, much more the conditions
of symmetry, may fail to make a strong appeal.   The
effects of present causes are so distant that they do not
seem real and unavoidable. Therefore, whatever the
pupil's ability or lack of ability to form and carry out
projects directed toward health, strength, and symmetry,
the teacher must not swerve from the known requirements of what might be called the laws of future welfare.

As scientific research increases our knowledge of
these laws, the area that we are under obligation to

[1] The fact has been communicated to me by an eminent orthopedist.

control grows larger, and the number of processes that are necessary, even though the young can have little knowledge or appreciation of them, increases. A certain private school causes every pupil to be examined periodically with reference to the physical factors that determine health, growth, and symmetry of body. The pupil who comes nearest of all the group to fulfilling the ideal of physical perfection is found, nevertheless, to be using one foot in such a way as to create danger of "flat-foot" in later life. The staff, therefore, decides that this child, for the sake of her future, must take corrective exercises now. How the required exercises in this instance were related to the project principle I shall tell after a little; at the present moment let us contemplate simply the fact that children whom we are accustomed to think of as so healthy and normal that they need no attention or control may in reality require much. Law is as minute, and as implacable, in the psycho-physical organism as it is in an explosives factory.

When certain boys became interested in guinea pigs, many phases of the educative project were promptly in evidence. Here was a self-chosen end, and here were forethought; planning and construction of pens; the daily routine of feeding the pets and cleaning the pens; discrimination of strains as to color, weight, and form; breeding for a particular type, with resulting knowledge of sex and of heredity; co-operation in study and in execution of plans. At the height of the interest the boys were certain that there was "money in it." Didn't fancy pigs bring as much as a dollar and a half? For days one boy insisted that he must have one of them for breeding purposes; he could easily get the money back by selling the offspring. But suddenly the bottom dropped out. "We're going to stop raising guinea pigs," said one of the boys. "The fad is over [in the towns 'round about], and there's no money in it any longer." How slow children are to realize the force of economic laws, and yet how important it is that these laws should have a right part in educational projects.

To get up early, climb to the hilltop, build a campfire, see the sun rise, and in this setting talk over some of their shortcomings with a teacher-leader—this was the spontaneous project of "the dormitory." When the eastern sky began to turn from gray to gold, "Boom, boom, boom" went the tom-tom as the procession of happy penitents started—happy because they had found a pleasing way to right a wrong that they had committed. But alas, how tangled together are right and wrong! Near by were families and small children who had a right to their morning sleep. This right had been recognized in a school rule against making noise before the regular rising hour, but the rule was forgotten, and so a second wrong had to be righted. This "had to be" was an educational imperative. For the sake of the offenders even more than for the sake of a handful of persons who might lose a half-hour of sleep, it was essential that law, in the form of a school regulation, should find a place in pupil projects.

A troop of youngsters goes into a forest bent upon the laudable educative purpose of building a log cabin. Selecting a fit site upon rising ground close to a brook, they begin to fell the necessary trees. Hereupon the owner appears and strenuously objects to their proceeding. They argue, perhaps truly, that he has more trees than he needs, that the forest will be benefited by thinning out, and that it is important to them to become masters of woodcraft. But the owner—unreasonably, perhaps—invokes his right under the law, and by threat of compulsion he puts an end to their project.[1] Here a law of the state rather than the purpose of the young determines the course of the project, and thereby compulsion of this type becomes the most important educative factor in the situation—the most important as measured by effectiveness, not necessarily by wholesomeness, for there is no doubt that the first conscious contacts of the young with common and statute law often train them in lawlessness.

A sixth-grade class was discussing a proposal to take part with the rest of the school in helping a neighboring day nursery. Some of the children argued that they had heard "day nursery" until they were tired of it; their parents were helping, anyway, and something more interesting could be found to do. "But," said one little debater, "somebody's got to do it, for the nursery really needs more income. It lacks this, and this, and this." Seeing that they could not agree, the children turned to the teacher for guidance. He suggested that a committee be appointed for further study of the situation in the hope that some action might be suggested that all could accept. The little chairman appointed as one member of the committee the boy who had most strenuously opposed doing anything for the nursery. On a subsequent day the committee reported substantially as follows: "Of

[1] This supposititious case arises out of my observation of the gruesome maiming and destruction of trees by boys' axes in public woodlands and privately owned groves in and near New York City.

course we've got to do *something*, and if we're going to do
anything it ought to be large enough to do credit to
the class. We recommend an appropriation of $5.00."
The report was unanimously adopted, and thereby the
class did more for the nursery than the teacher himself
would have advised. Let us consider for a moment what
is indicated by the words of the committee: "Of course
we've got to do something." What is this "got to,"
this law that is enforceable only through the free consent
of those whom it commands? Let us call it, broadly,
moral law.

The obligation was brought home in this instance by
two main processes: Contemplation of the situation at
the nursery, which aroused intelligent sympathy and
brought into action a habit already formed of helping
neighbors who needed help, and the pressure of opinion
in the immediate school environment. Now, these two
phases of moral law—appreciation of ends, and the
force of social customs, standards, and opinions—do not
bear any constant ratio to each other in conduct. Sometimes the directly felt value of something passes over into
action without reinforcement from social sentiment;
sometimes a standard enforces itself almost entirely
through imitation and other forms of suggestion, so
that one acts morally, and forms habits of so acting,
with next to no satisfactions except those that arise
from social approval and disapproval. At a later point
we shall have to wrestle with the significance of this
distinction for educational theory. What is the relative
value, we shall ask, of projects in which morally good
action arises in response to a perceived and appreciated
need or possible value, as compared with projects in

which moral action consists in conforming to a social standard without fresh contacts with the ends that justify it?

A knot of boys was conversing in a moderate tone when one spoke up vehemently: "But, is it fair?" He had encountered law in still another sense, the law of the ideal. Another instance is that of a youngster who had been doing a certain duty reluctantly, often receiving pay for doing it. On one occasion he suddenly said to his mother: "I'll do it, and you needn't pay me for it." In his Sunday school he had caught a glimpse of an ideal relationship of boys to mothers, and the ideal had taken hold of him as a law. Did you ever observe a group of pupils deliberating upon the question of adopting the "honor system" in examinations? If so, probably you witnessed a struggle between the claims of an ideal and the counter-claims of the actual, between "as it should be" and "it is too difficult."

We do not stretch the proprieties of language when we speak of the ideal as law, for persistent idealizing marks the strivings of humanity as truly as does legislation. We are summoned from within to a sensitive and generous living that outruns all formal rules and regulations. It outruns public opinion, too, being more fine in its discriminations and exacting in its expectations; it outruns even what goes under the name of morality. This paradox, that we recognize a higher law within and yet beyond our laws, a higher self within yet above the self of each of us, a something more moral than morality, is interpreted by religion in the thought that God is a morally creative will working within humanity throughout its evolution.

This is not the place to press this or any other interpretation, but it is the place to contemplate the fact of law in the form of ideals. It is true that injurious things have been done in the name of idealism, or of moral authority, or of religion, but let us not offset error by folly—the folly of ignoring and doing nothing about one of the great areas of human motivation. It is true that the nature of ideals has been mistakenly conceived, and that we need on all accounts to realize that they arise out of the actual, that they are historically conditioned, that they require revision, and that sometimes they stand in the way of vigorous grappling with actualities; but the fact that ideals are thus human proves, not their powerlessness, but their power. If realism should forget this, it would be insufficiently realistic; if pragmatism should forget, it would be insufficiently pragmatic.

The point of this for us teachers just now is not that we should choose appropriate ideals and proceed to "impress" them upon the minds of the young; not that we should put the name of God into the Constitution, and the Bible and worship into tax-supported schools; not that we should slacken the pace of our movement to bring education closer to the practical requirements of life; but first of all that we should recognize the plain fact that pupils do form ideals of great import whether with or without our help, and that ideals represent a species of motivation, an actual or possible inner law in projects.

An adolescent girl's *journal intime* that I was permitted to read in manuscript sometime ago revealed this situation: She was the daughter of a widow in straitened circumstances. She loved her mother with the same

intensity with which she loved a certain young man—
no, with greater intensity. For she not only dreamed
of projects for earning money that should relieve her
mother from the necessity of grinding labor, but she
assisted her mother in this labor, and in addition carried
through the project of secretly writing a story for
publication. The details of her prolonged labor under
cover of night, and of the crushing disillusionment when
her manuscript was rejected, form a human document
of rarely moving interest. The intermixture of reals
and ideals, of dreams and hard work, is remarkable.
Yet it does but paint in unusually vivid colors factors
that enter into the experience of all of us. And not least
among the practical idealists is he who seeks to awaken
society from an illusory idealism, to bring experience
down to solid ground, to induce men to see whatever is
seeable and then ask themselves: "In this situation, what
do I really want?" To insist that the good is not static,
and that the idea and the expectation of change be incorporated into morals, religion, and education is as much
as to say that ideals are the proper masters of the actual,
and that they are of the very essence of the project.

We have now glanced at six phases of law as an actual
factor in the projects of the young, whether we will or no,
and whether either pupil or teacher is aware of it or not.
They, alongside of definitely conscious purposes, are so
many determiners of the educational outcome of school
projects. These six are:

1. *Natural laws.*—They represent what can or cannot
be, and hence determine success or failure, either because
of the nature of materials or because of the nature and
condition of the pupil. These laws determine, likewise,

by-products in body and mind, desirable or not, and whether aimed at or not.

2. *Teacher-laws.*—Based upon insight (which the pupil may or may not possess) into the conditions of present and future welfare, teacher-laws see to it that these conditions shall prevail in the situations in which the pupil is placed.

3. *Economic laws.*—They apply within a considerable range of the motivation and conduct even of small children; often determine success or failure; and likewise affect many human relations.

4. *Common and statute law.*—It is a compulsory factor in the experience of young and old, and the conscious contacts of the young with it determine important social attitudes.

5. *Moral law.*—It appears in the two forms of the *good*, or values that depend upon me, and *obligation*, or the pressure within me of the demands or expectations of others, whether human or divine. In both forms it is, of course, a factor in the purposes of the young.

6. *Ideals as laws.*—Being most completely self-imposed, ideals may be regarded as the last steps in self-assertion, but as they actually are imposed, and as they cost labor and even what men call self-sacrifice, they may well be called laws.

CHAPTER II

NATURAL LAW BOTH OPENS AND CLOSES DOORS

Sometimes it is necessary to utter a truism in order to give the right setting to what is not truistic. In the present instance the truism is that within every purposeful act of teacher or pupil, natural law is a co-determinant of all that occurs. Needless to say, perhaps, I am now using the term "natural law" in the popular sense that permits one to distinguish men as thinking, free-acting beings from nature as a mechanism. The laws of this mechanism appear within our very own activities in the material in which one works (my own act adjusting itself to the nature and processes of the material); in the tool that one uses; in the energies that one turns to account— the weight of the hammer, the heat of the forge, the actinic rays of the sun; and in environing conditions that affect the human organism, as atmosphere, temperature, illumination, bacteria, and distracting sights and sounds. These things obviously have much to do with what shall be wrought in the materials and in the child. For short, we may say that natural law prescribes the extent to which a given desire is attainable; if attainable at all, the cost in terms of materials consumed, labor, risks of failure of the project, and risks of pain, sickness, or deformity; and, whether attainable or not, what the educational gains and losses will be, not only in the way of intelligence and skill, but also in the way of mindsets. This is the truism.

What is not a truism is that society and the school are facing a part of this truth about law less squarely than another part. Let us note the ways in which, in childhood as well as in maturity, we consciously encounter the something that in maturity we call "natural law." Nature often presents herself as a blank "Thou canst not" that paralyzes the project attitude. Who has not seen a child weep over the refractoriness of some material, or over the recurrence of an obnoxious event, or over the inco-ordination of his own muscles? On the other hand, nature invites us with a "Thou canst," her laws appearing now not as a restriction upon the project attitude, but as a stimulus of it. Have you ever seen a boy discover the water-wheel possibility of a brook, or even the echo-possibility of a hill? But, in the third place, natural laws are so intertwined with one another that whenever we accept nature's invitation to form a project we invariably become subject to some further law that henceforth restricts the scope of our effective choices. Whenever we enter an open door, some door closes. There is set before us, say, a varied table from which we eat and drink what we will, but the food and drink, once taken into the body, become subject to chemical changes, and we ourselves inevitably become subject to them. A child can saw a board in two, or divide a length of cloth, but he can never thereafter recover the board or the length of cloth—they are gone forever. This third aspect of law is the one to which we give the least attention.

The experience of free activity in a project leads on, then, to experience of restriction and limitation that otherwise would not exist for us. We never can reverse

any process so as to go back and "begin all over again."
Yet, under the illusion that we can at any time make
a fresh start by merely reversing something that we call
our own will, we consume materials that cannot be
replaced, repel personalities that never come our way
again, make psychic wounds that leave a scar even if they
heal, reduce our own power to achieve, or even put to
sleep our desire to do so. Thus, though we are fairly
aware, in our projects, of the "Thou canst" and of the
"Thou canst not," we do not with clearness recognize
the "Thou canst, but. . . . ."

This sounds, perhaps, like a homily upon adult life.
But in fact there is no break in this respect between
childhood and maturity. It is strictly true that "we
pass this way but once." The better we know the psychology of childhood the more certain it becomes that
early experiences are important determinants of the whole
course of one's life. Anything like this was hidden from
the old rationalistic psychology of ideas. It allowed one
to think (whether or not this was directly asserted) that
the essential activities of mind are those that appear in
its ideas; that ideas, though they originate in sense
experience, detach themselves from their sense basis
and become, as it were, free-floating entities, and that,
therefore, one might at any time become any sort of
person by having the appropriate thoughts, and might
thus take advantage of any resource that nature contains.
Hence, child experience, whether in health or in disease,
was not regarded as significant. The play of children,
their contacts with nature and with people, their likes and
dislikes, their pains and pleasures, their emotional up-
heavals, their enterprises and achievements, even their

curiosity, were regarded as temporary matters, all to be left behind in the journey toward manhood.

We are now recovering from this disastrous error, just as we are recovering from the parallel notion that certain diseases, as measles, are to be expected in childhood, and are nothing more than an inconvenience of the period. The parallel is remarkably close. Just as measles may have after-effects that were unsuspected, so the whole psycho-physical process in the early years produces mind-sets that later in life are designated as bent, peculiarity, disposition, idiosyncrasy, gift, natural aversion, "complex," genius for, character, personality. We know that childish whims, fears, tantrums, sex-interests and reactions, social attachments and repulsions, sense of success or of failure, sense of strength or of weakness, satisfied or baffled curiosity, feeling of freedom or of restraint—we know that all these have after-effects of great importance. Thus, when nature entices us to enter any open door—to enter it either voluntarily or impulsively—she closes doors the instant we enter. Any act, any experience, limits the remaining alternatives in some specific manner.

Of natural law as opening doors of opportunity, of the wonders of control that are rapidly coming to view, so much has been said that little needs to be added here. This little, however, is by no means unimportant. It is twofold. First, who is to wield this enormously increasing control of natural resources that the sciences are making possible? Second, to what ends are these resources to be applied? As yet we have only a partial answer to either of these questions. It is evident that direct control of natural resources by individuals and small aggregations of men is passing into indirect and diminished control by the many and enormously increased control by the few who manage the ever more organized industries and businesses. The ends to which our augmented powers are being directed are in major degree the increase of power on the part of those who already have the most, and in minor degree the improvement of human life. This is reflected in an interesting manner in the federal income-tax law, which exempts from taxation gifts for religious, philanthropic, and educational purposes to the extent of only 15 per cent of one's income. That is, if one gives away 30 per cent of one's income instead of 15 per cent, the second 15 per cent is not exempted, because this would increase the tax of those who give away a smaller proportion of their income. To him that withholdeth, more withholding; from him that giveth most generously, a second giving in the form of taxation is required.

Law as invitation to power is bound to play a great rôle in school projects. Rightly so. The fascinated child of the future school is to be, not the amused child, not the passively appreciative child, but the child who experiences increase of power through scientific laws and processes. What, then, shall he experience as to the distribution of power, and what shall he experience as to the ends to be served by it? Natural law opens doors, but doors to what? It is certain that pupil projects will give some answer to this question. The answer will come whether teachers plan for it or not. It will come from the customs of society, from the common speech of men, from examples of men of power. Therefore, it is essential that teachers should definitely assume responsibility for this inevitable phase of school projects. Upon this point more will be said when we reach our discussion of economic laws as factors of projects.

In view of the restrictive and door-closing aspect of natural law, one would naturally assume that the whole movement from infancy through childhood and adolescence into maturity should include, project-fashion, the discipline of self-restriction—better, perhaps, self-organization and self-balance—as well as the discipline of self-expansion and outward achievement. Surely, one would say, any people that enjoys even a moderate measure of schooling will be schooled in this respect. Yet a dispassionate survey of our society will show that this is not the case. Here is a suggestion toward such a survey:

We know far better how to heap up resources than how to increase our joys even were our resources unlimited.

We are so absorbed in the machinery of life that, instead of running it, we are run by it.

We are increasing the speed of life, but we do not know whither we are actually going, or whither we really care to go.

Men live wastefully. They strive to make ends meet by increasing their income far more than by regulating their expenditures.

Men live disproportionately, not seeing great things as great and small things as small. For the most part they do not even look to see.

Men live below their capacity. On the whole they do not shirk work, but they neglect the prior choices upon which the level and the meaning of work depend.

Most of us violate the plain dictates of hygiene, and as a consequence rarely maintain for long a reasonably high physiological level.

In spite of the rudimentary knowledge of eugenics that is within everybody's reach, almost unregulated preference controls mating, good stocks are constantly diluted, and society is burdened with defectives.

Marital happiness is sought where, in the nature of the case, it cannot be found.

Most parents bring up their children by impulse and guess-work, yet believe that they really love their offspring.

Day by day the old, old story of self-indulgence that is self-defeating and self-destroying repeats itself.

Multitudes of young persons, though they are desirous of success in their occupations, constantly do the very things that prevent or restrict success.

The country is sprinkled over with investment schemes into which intelligent men and women—some of them teachers—are pouring money that will never return.

In industrial relations, and in international matters, our great men are desperately engaged in gathering figs from thistles.

Thus, untold mental and bodily vigor, and untold natural resources are being expended upon what the "gentle pessimist" of the Old Testament calls "vanity, and a striving after wind." One might ask whether men really know that two plus two equals four, or believe that "Whatsoever a man soweth, that shall he also reap." For, in every one of these items knowledge adequate to show a better way is somewhere available.

Educative processes of the right sort could prevent a large proportion of this waste of opportunity, of happiness, of vigor, and of resources. The young *drift* into permanently injurious, or permanently inferior habits; they do it without evil intent, and indeed often at the very time that they are strenuously pursuing educational or occupational ends. Men fail to grasp the good that life holds out to them, not in any large measure because they deliberately or even consciously turn aside from any wisdom that they ever possessed, but chiefly because, in childhood and youth, they had too few of the experiences that could start them on the road to wisdom. Either a habit of thinking of life as within natural law is not formed, or natural law is presented too exclusively under the aspect of opportunity for satisfying desires—as matters most commonly stand, opportunity for controlling things and men so as to increase our income, and thereby increase our ability to get what we want. Of law as pitilessly defeating our desires, of law as preventing us from having desirable desires, and of law as imposing undesirable by-consequences even when we get, what we think we want—of this how little do we learn until too late!

Here is an unsolved problem of teaching. If we may distinguish between a narrow positive wisdom that is concerned with how to achieve a few obvious ends, and negative wisdom (what desires not to follow, either because they cannot achieve their objects, or because achievement is too costly), then we may say that education is far better developed in the direction of narrow positive wisdom than in the direction of even the broadest and most important negative wisdom. Our most effective teaching concerns the tools and processes for achieving the conventional ends of life—the ends toward which one moves with the least demand for discrimination.

That negative wisdom, however vitally needed, lags behind conventional positive wisdom is due to an inherent difficulty that has a psychological basis. The restrictive aspect of law is the one that children and adults, too, least readily appreciate. To a child a jack-knife is a tool that cuts sticks; that it cuts fingers also is in the shadowy background of thought if it is there at all. To adults automobiles are things with which one can "get there"; how slow we are to take in the fact that they slay and maim as in a battle. To a child a deep pool in a stream means fishing or swimming, not possible drowning. To adults a big pool or lake is a thing toward which water flows, therefore a convenient destination for sewage, but likewise a reservoir whence water can be procured, and hence a convenient source for the water supply of a town. How long it takes even intelligent citizens, in spite of abundant knowledge of typhoid, to make up their minds not to drink dilute sewage.

Anyone who thinks that the necessary work of education in respect to negative wisdom can be done by saying "Don't do this" and "Don't do that" is welcome to his thoughts. Less unwise are teachers who rely upon abstract scientific intelligence to solve our problem. For genuine intelligence—which is not to be confused with correct concatenation of words in an examination— is surely handy in emergencies. But wisdom implies more than this, even a habit of seeing what is needed, and a habit of thinking of the sciences in their relation to needs. The problem for the school, then, is that of producing cultivated repulsions as well as attractions— cultivated in the sense that seeds of likes and dislikes are sown and watered and the resulting plants weeded; attractions and repulsions cultivated in the further sense that they are brought into relation to known causes and effects. In a word, our schools must do more than they are now doing in the way of negative—that is to say, self-restrictive—discipline of the project type.

But we have to face the fact that some things that are in intimate causal relations to our desires must not

be learned by children through their own experience of the effects. Being poisoned by poison ivy is an effective, but too costly, way for a Boy Scout to learn how to care for himself on a "hike" into the hills. Rattlesnake fangs can teach, after a fashion, but the fashion is not a good one. What not to eat is not to be learned by eating it, for unwholesome diet creates an appetite for itself, and besides it reduces the physical tone that is required for education generally. There are fields into which the pupil should be induced, as far as possible through his own conviction, never to enter. As in diet, so in respect to the sex appetite, it is important to go right the first time and every time. The eyes need very early to be protected from misuse, even misuse suggested and urged by worthwhile motives, such as interest in good literature. For the sake of protecting myself and others from infection, it is necessary not to trifle or dally even a single time with this or that attractive and innocent-looking situation.

These samples are selected from the field of hygiene. If we understood mental and moral causation as well as we understand the body, we should possibly find parallel acts and experiences, usually called mental, that likewise maim and destroy. What is the effect of the first success in deliberate and planned cribbing in an examination? Let us ignore for the moment the little deceptions into which pupils impulsively slip; let us consider only real projects in deception. Satisfactions of various kinds ensue upon success—escape from a disagreeable study by finishing it; the social standing and the opening doors guaranteed by a good mark; approbation of parents; mastering, or at least defeating, a teacher who thinks himself the master; the sense of power that comes from doing a difficult thing; admiration from fellow-pupils for one's adroitness. From a single experience of this kind a serious, permanent set might result. Are we as sure of the effect of any counter-education that we know how to provide as we are of this set? Even if such a case is not quite parallel to the permanent injury of a bodily organ, should not schools fortify pupils, through projects *anti*, against the first temptation to crib? Wide-awake teachers know that in various parts of the country most of the pupils of certain grades acquire subterranean information about facts and methods of cribbing, and are subject to the influence of subterranean standards *ad hoc*.

Whether it is similarly important to forestall all experience of gambling is worth considering. A parent said, "My son of fourteen is absorbed in a form of poker that is played by boys in our neighborhood. What will be the effect?" The stakes were not money, or anything of value beyond the fun of the moment and the satisfactions that arise from the possession of skill. But the well-known mental processes of the grown-up poker-gambler were cultivated, the technic of a gambling game was learned, and certain of the grown-up gambler's joys were had. This suggests the following question: If the natural laws of habit-formation are what we take them to be, and if gambling, as most of us believe, is a social evil, is there any way to keep the young from ever falling into it unless education includes projects *anti*?

What is to be the relation of school projects to the failures of adults—the foolishness or the wickedness, the tragedy or the emptiness, of misguided or unguided individual lives, and the wastes, the futilities, and the injustices of social organizations? Thus far the school activities to which the name project is approvingly given are those that typify, and if possible participate in, the worthwhile activities of adults. Examine specimen projects almost anywhere, and you will find plans for enabling children to have the satisfying experience of success in doing something that is inherently worth doing. Such positive projects should undoubtedly form the main staple of school procedure, but they should contain or be supplemented by project factors specifically directed toward the avoidance or prevention of ills.

It is true that in the execution of positive projects dissatisfactions are bound to occur, with the result of teaching some negative wisdom. Inaccurate measurements, haste, carelessness with tools, untidiness, social friction, unfavorable judgment upon the product passed by teacher and fellow-pupils—all these help to steady a pupil's will. Yet such defeats, pains, and negative wisdom as these are altogether minor and accessory; the end here aimed at by the pupils does not touch even the borderline of the false conventional aims or the uneconomical and destructive processes that these same pupils will encounter in adult life when they engage in the same sort of positive activity.

Instances in point might be gathered from many parts of our economic, political, and social life. Take, for example, our wasteful exploitation of natural resources. Wood-working projects in the school are likely to take timber for granted; it is one of nature's open doors. Yet timber, looked at soberly and socially, means that our wonderful forests, once a public domain existing for the benefit of the people, are being destroyed for private profit.   How many of us know how long it takes patient nature to make a pine tree?   Once I counted the rings of a smallish Norway pine that was about to be used for temporary piling in connection with the elevation of a railroad track.   They numbered 175.   A nearby maple of similar size had only a hundred less rings.   The larger white pine trees are found to have 250 to 300 rings. A board, then, according to the way you look at it, may be either a potential shelf, or a specimen of nature's artistry, or a summons to stop the waste, rapidly approaching exhaustion, of our forests.

It is easy for school projects to awaken admiration for works of man that are only partly admirable.   Our tall buildings may serve as a convenient example. The coming of steel seems at first sight to give us a solution (in part) for the problem of rising ground-rents in our cities.   For, by increasing the height of our buildings from four or six stories to twenty, we multiply several fold the amount of business that can be done upon a given number of square feet of land.   Yet, in city after city, streets and sidewalks that accommodated the people under the old conditions can do so no longer— the capacity of the tall buildings outruns the capacity of the streets.   So, we build subways; but at one end of them we erect more tall buildings, at the other end of them more apartment houses, so that shortly the subways and the streets both are congested.   Then we build more subways, only to repeat the problem.   Yes, great is steel, but. . . . . Magnificently impressive are our tall buildings, but. . . . .

A century or more ago the westward-moving population came upon a river that offered wondrous water-power. Here were three water-falls, two of them of great height. What should be done with such a river but build mills and mill-races along its banks and in its gorges? Result, a large and thriving city, but the magnificent old river flows, sewage-laden, between the repulsive back walls of factories and storehouses, while the populace pants for open spaces and natural beauty. Natural law opens doors, but whenever we enter she closes some door.

Here, then, in a nutshell, is the educational situation and the resulting problem: Both nature and the conventions of society in its dealing with natural resources invite and urge us, both children and adults, into projects that are either impracticable or too costly—projects that first yield satisfaction but afterward restrict, impoverish, overburden, or injure us. Saying "Don't" is not an effective way to counteract the readiness of children and youth to respond to such allurement, or to prevent them from admiring unduly human works whose size and glitter conceal the revenges of law upon man's projects. Some help, but not enough, comes from knowledge of the causal relations involved. Therefore something in the nature of projects *anti*, or at least contra-conventional, appears to be required, or possibly projects that are two-edged, both *pro* and *anti*. An early task of progressive teachers might well be some exploration in this direction.

CHAPTER III

THE PROJECT AS THE METHOD OF
NATURE

Thus far we have treated natural law as popular thought treats it, namely, as playing a part alongside of the human will. That we have not completely or consistently adhered to this point of view, however, is in the nature of things. For law is within us as well as around about us, and the laws that are within connect our activities with the whole system of nature. The project itself is a natural phenomenon. An ancient one, too, not a flower that has just bloomed for the first time. A child's persistent exploration of objects with hands and eyes; his insistent questions; his climbing, running away, doing something to see what will happen; his fondness for making things, and his pride in his products; his desire to have a part in the doings of his elders; his impulse to accumulate, sort, and classify things; his efforts to master animals, other children, and adults; his emulation of skill and prowess—this is a partial indication of how the sap of human nature constantly thrusts out project buds.

That project method in teaching depends upon and carries out this project impulse in our nature has been sufficiently said by others. But insufficient attention has been given to the fact that education as such selects between what I have called project buds, predestining some of them to free development and others to arrest or extirpation. Now, the situations in which pupils are to be placed are far more minutely and continuously scrutinized by project teaching than by the methods that it is displacing. Hence we might say that in the project method nature turns upon herself more discriminatingly than before, and grows cautious even of her own project impulses. We have just seen that nature, as well as the conventions and customs of society, often urges us into disastrous projects, sometimes miseducating us and then leaving us incapable of re-education. As a consequence, the suggestion was made that we should have in the schools projects *anti* as well as *pro*. This conclusion rests securely upon the grounds already adduced. But the grounds are broader and deeper still, and they require something still more radical. This I shall endeavor to show in the present chapter. Taking for granted the beneficent training that nature provides through our multitude of project impulses, let us squarely face once more the inherently and inevitably injurious activities, purposeful as well as impulsive, into which she leads us, and then ask what significance they have for the theory of the project.

Using the term "nature" in the broad sense that includes the whole of human nature, we may say that the misdirected energies of men, the monumental failures of individuals and of societies, the wrongs that groan their way through history and still cry to heaven for redress, all are natural expressions of men in natural environments, all are phases of the project in developed form.

In a scientific age these things glare at us with hot scorn. For, apart from the shortness of life, the major woes of mankind are no longer those occasioned by natural calamities—storms, earthquakes, avalanches, droughts, inescapable plagues—but those occasioned by us men through our failure to apply our knowledge where it will do the most good.   And our curse is not inactivity, for we are full of action, such as it is.   A vast proportion of our activity is organized, too, systematized, and directed to desired ends.   Human life is not chaos, it is not anarchy, it is not beastlike obedience to instinct; it is, on the whole, project life.   But something is wrong, or many things are wrong, with our projects.   Millions of children are undernourished in countries that are rich and resourceful;   they are undernourished not because we cannot feed them, but because we are busy with projects that do not include their welfare.   The pitiful education that the public schools are offering to most of the children of this country is not due to inability to provide better education, but to preoccupation with projects that seem more important.   So with municipal misrule.   We could have honest administration of our cities if we wanted it intensely—we surely know enough —but we do not make it a part of our business, that is, our project.

And what shall we say of the mountainous failure that is now in the minds of all of us?   Consider, for a moment, the significance of war merely as a project— as a whole-hearted, purposeful, social activity—without regard to its justification or lack of justification.   Never did human beings guide the forces of nature into thought-determined channels upon such a scale, with such rapidity, and with such precision, as in the Great War.   Never did the capacity of men to work together in great masses so clearly reveal itself.   Here, measured by the natural forces and the men involved, is the greatest demonstration we have ever had of the project capacity of men. Never again let it be said that intelligence that can wage war in this manner cannot put an end to war! The reason why the end of war does not come is that men are engaged in projects that seem more important than insurance against international conflict. "While thy servant was busy about many things, behold, he was gone." Nay, this is only the lesser part of the truth. The secret, formerly known to the few, became a possession of the many during the Great War, that modern wars do not happen chiefly because we are absent-mindedly employed upon something entirely unrelated thereto, but because we carry on industry and commerce by a species of minor war that leads on toward major conflicts between nations. Our everyday projects are themselves infected with the virus.

The popular excuse for ancient man-made evils is that strong and ineradicable impulses of human nature obstruct and defeat reason. That is, the impulses of the other fellow, of course! Said Mr. A to Mr. B: "Human nature being what it is, war is inevitable." Said Mr. B to Mr. A: "You yourself are able and willing to live at peace with all mankind, aren't you?" "O, yes!" replied Mr. A. "How does it happen, Mr. A," rejoined B, "that you consider yourself so much better than the rest of mankind?" Thus do we excuse the shortcomings of our projects, our definitely purposed activities, by alleging some weakness of human nature in the rest of the world!

But this self-deception, too, is a part of nature's way of starting projects and making them go. Her versatility is astonishing. Through our natural interests she teaches us to sow and reap; then she adds a farm tractor to the processes of wheat-growing; and then she devises a submarine to destroy the wheat. One and the same subtle sex interest teaches now how to make faces bloom by intelligently directed diet and exercise, then how to make them bloom by intelligently directed powder-puffs and lip-sticks. Doubtless nature is bent upon teaching, and she does it by the project method, but what is her curriculum?

A striking phase of this situation is the fact, already touched upon, that adults as well as children are more responsive to opportunities for action than experience warrants them in being. The likelihood of discomfort at the end of a project does not control our conduct as much as equal likelihood of success and satisfaction. The action's the thing. A well-known example is the slowness of men to submit to control by their own reason in matters of sanitation and hygiene. We are so busy, so full of projects, that we do not have time to make ourselves either safe or comfortable! Other examples are "get-rich-quick" schemes, and . . . . well, our whole economic fever. For surely we are not in the business of manufacturing human happiness or character.

In human conduct, then, plus A and minus A do not cancel each other. Equal magnitudes, placed in opposite scale pans, do not leave the beam horizontal. Some irrational factor, we infer, must infest the project attitude as such, a factor that pulls us toward action per se rather than toward rational good.

This over-readiness is reinforced, or revealed, by three interlacing psychic processes: (1) There is the fact, long recognized under other names, that we now call "rationalization." We initiate courses of action, we know not why, or only half know, and then find reasons for them. Having found reasons for them, we stiffen them, systematize them, and pursue them dogmatically—and sincerely. Whatever we are voluntarily engaged in, and much that is involuntary, we tend to "rationalize." (2) Everyone who is not morbidly depressed represents the past in his memory, not just as it was experienced, but with modifications in the interest of his self-esteem. The errors of our memory are not hit-and-miss; they are like loaded dice. And the tendency of this irrational factor is to the justification and hence continuance of courses of action already entered upon. (3) Precisely in line with this is the experimentally known fact that we forget unpleasant (or restraining) experiences more readily than pleasant (or stimulating) ones. Our "forgettery" as well as our memory favors action more than it favors discrimination.

Thus does the human mind gaze with a magnifying glass upon its successes, both past and prospective, and with a reversed lens upon its failures, both past and prospective. Our nature has a skew; we are bent first toward irrational risks, and then away from clear consciousness of the losses that our foolish conduct brings upon us.

Let us speak more literally. Action as such is satisfying whenever the organism is in fit condition for action. This is one of the constants that deflect the scales in which we weigh our projects, whether they are already accomplished, or in progress, or merely contemplated. Again, this satisfaction in the mere fact that our powers are in exercise is enhanced when the realization is brought home that these powers are *my own*, or that *I* am controlling something or somebody. Milton's hero, Satan, would rather rule in hell than serve in heaven. Just so, a child will weep over an act that he feels is forced upon him, but glory in the same act when he feels that it is an achievement of his own. Thus it is that sometimes, paradoxically, children experiment to see how much they can endure, and even adults not seldom certify to themselves their own strength by voluntarily creating hardships. If we were to reinstate the old hedonistic calculus, we should say that the immediate satisfaction of action as such (favorable organic conditions being granted), and especially the immediate satisfaction of self-activity, is sufficient to overcome an appreciable amount of immediate discomfort, a large amount of remote discomfort even though it be certain, and an almost unlimited amount of remote discomfort if it is only probable, not certain. All this obviously tends to introduce an illusory factor into our projects.

The explanation of this peculiar, deep-seated weighting of action as such is found in nature's primordial method of sustaining, perpetuating, and evolving species. Action, abundant and varied, though it means death to many members of a species, is the way in which nature makes sure that at least some members shall hit upon the means of sustenance and strength. She makes good the enormous losses that are incident to this process by a compensating fecundity. It is true that the evolution of specialized organs and instincts is accompanied by reduction in the range of the risks taken, and by corresponding reduction in fecundity; but the method of hitting the mark now and then by firing a great many shots in a general direction remains in operation in every species. Even in the human species, which has the advantage of insurance by means of analysis and foresight, the older and more expensive sort of insurance is still in operation.

It operates unless it is resisted "head on," that is, by rational self-control. The marks of rational living all center around a certain checking of ourselves. Thus: (1) We postpone action while we analyze a situation so as to determine upon a more specific objective. (2) We rearrange the causal factors, both outside ourselves and within ourselves. (3) We reorganize our habits so as to utilize the right causes with the least deflection by irrelevant impulses, and so as to keep us going right even when we do not stop to think. (4) We protect from themselves individuals, as children, who are not yet capable of this self-checking. (5) We perpetuate the controls thus resulting by incorporating them into systems of education.

In our species, this, the latest-developed method of adjustment, exists side by side with the primordial biological method. To some extent they can be harmonized, as in supervised play. Yet they do not coalesce. Far from it; they are so antithetical to each other that one of the chief functions of reason and of education is to displace the wasteful and painful adjustment processes of pre-rational nature by the more economical processes of nature-become-rational in man.

This brings it to pass that rational living is possible only at the cost of internal strains. Plato is not exactly popular at present; nevertheless his figure of the unruly steeds and the stiff reins that have to be held upon them seems made to fit modern conditions. And it fits other conditions than the overabundant sex urge that makes us so much trouble. It holds, likewise, for the group of impulsions that underlie, first, the securing of food, and then the accumulation of possessions. Whatever the part played by native greed, rivalry, and the instinct of mastery, on the one hand, and by desire for food and for the security of self and offspring, or by the play impulse (business is a game) on the other, our economic activity is clearly not adjusted to our needs, is not guided by foresight of them in any such measure as would necessitate the judgment that we are rational creatures. The chief sign of growing rationality in our economic order is not its enormous and complicated organization of resources and of human power, but the internal strain that it is beginning to feel with respect to its own motives and results. Our economic system is an unruly steed just as truly as sex. For our whole civilization is taking as a self-evident good economic processes, privileges, and results that mix good and bad, justice and injustice, more abundant life and impoverished life. If, then, we desire to educate through projects that involve economic consciousness, we must incorporate in these projects a critique of the economic order. Rational economic living is possible only at the cost of internal economic strains.

There is an old and popular belief that parental impulse in and of itself is wise. Especially the mother-heart is by nature endowed with insight, or with instinct that takes the place of insight. The mother, even without scientific study of children or of education, is held to be the best possible nurse and teacher. The grain of gold that this popular opinion contains makes one loath to attack it. There is, undoubtedly, moral value, primal social constructiveness, in the experience of family affection, especially if it issues in a genuinely co-operative scheme of living. But this "if" is a large one, and the possibilities of unwise and ineffective affection are legion. If parental affection were wise, it would give the parent no rest until he learned what science has to say as to the nutrition and physical care of the child; as to how habits are formed, and what habits need to be formed or avoided in childhood; how to instruct children of different ages concerning sex; how to co-operate with the day school and the church school in their work of teaching; how to develop self-guidance in the child, and how at last to emancipate him from parental control. If parental affection were wise! What we see in most families is action, often genuinely planned action, based upon the fallacy that what I feel strongly must be so, especially if I act from affection. The result? Ask any teacher who knows intimately the life of children! Here, again, the project as the method of nature requires cautious scrutiny and deliberate checking.

Yet there is a certain amount of justice in the present reaction against the interpretation that Plato and a long line of Christian teachers have given to the division that is within us—the division that makes us human. They ascribed our trouble to the existence of a lower or sense stratum in our nature. Reason they thought of as a supernal essence against which sense is in constant rebellion. On the other hand, modern science finds in human nature no such break as this. Senses and intellect,

instinct and reason, bodily desires and spiritual aspira-
tions, all are phases of one whole. There is continuity
of process and—what is more important for our present
discussion—there is continuity of a dynamic sort. No
such thing as unmotived thought, passionless reason,
or self-evolved spiritual aspiration exists. We are
creatures with interests, and our interests envelop and
suffuse all that we are. We think not only with our
brain, but also with the autonomic system, and with our
glands of internal secretion. Out of this sense-rooted
endowment grows the best that we are in science, art,
morals, and religion as truly as the various degradations
that we fain would cover up.

This truth has consequences that our culture generally
has not perceived or desired to investigate. They would
shock a Plato. One of them is that, since the blood that
flows in science, invention, art, religion, and morals is
the very same blood that flows through our most untamed
impulses, even our superior guides for conduct are never
quite competent. This is true both of propositions or
maxims as guides and of men as guides. For the *meaning*
of a proposition or maxim never resides in the words, but
in the way they are taken, the setting they have in a
given order of society. "Thou shalt not steal" means
any one of several different and sometimes conflicting
standards. Think of the possible meanings of neighbor-
love that have scarcely begun to dawn upon those who
confess allegiance to the second great commandment.
As to men as guides for men, they cannot quite achieve
competence because they are swayed within themselves
by the very forces that they think to control. All
our superior men are influenced by what is temporary and

passing in the life about them. There are styles in science itself; art, as it is, is largely fashion; if you will give a concrete description of any moral or religious system, social psychology will tell you what stage or type of society it represents. As we have "period furniture" so also we have period culture even where we strive to achieve the fixed and eternal.

A second consequence is that we "rationalize" even reason itself wherever it anywhere concretely operates. We are overfond of our best, not merely of our worst! Our systematic overreadiness for action, and our over-readiness to persist in action that is once started, especially action that heightens our sense of self (individual or social), spreads through our higher as well as our lower projects. Hence, the project principle contains *within itself* a tendency to trust illusory hopes and to accept illusory successes.

But it is equally true that there is no insurance against such illusions except a deliberate insurance project, or rather, insurance factor in our projects. An insurance factor in the projects, not of some few leaders, but of all who form and execute any projects whatever. The need of checks and restrictions upon the generality of mankind has been recognized for thousands of years, and priests, philosophers, kings, and statesmen have been set apart as specialists in this work. Under this scheme, to speak broadly rather than exactly, the characteristic project of the common man is to control some part of the forces of nature, while the project of those set apart is to control the common man. Latterly the chief figure among the guides and shepherds of men has been the modern capitalist. Not only has his control of the

means of life for the multitude carried with it corresponding control of men, but it has begotten in him a
naïve certainty that he is a competent guide for the
masses. His naïveté is a capital example of the inherent
tendency to illusion in the project as such. Indeed, this
whole division of labor between the leader and the led
is saturated with it. Even if the division should be
found to rest upon some necessity in a historical situation,
the necessity does not alter the character of the fact, nor
lessen the need for relief from the remedy. In the nature
of the case, those whose project it is to guide the masses
overestimate their own wisdom and become victims
even of their own virtues. They are overready to guide,
and, having entered upon a policy, they "rationalize"
it. On the other hand, the masses who are thus con-
trolled, as soon as they are inured to the habit of it,
likewise "rationalize" their situation, and therefore
overestimate the wisdom of their guides.

Amazing is the strength of this self-deluding drive
within both the leaders and the led. Behold whither
the guides of civilization have conducted us—the capitalists, the statesmen, the men of science, the priests!
Yet these men show no signs of repentance, no lack of
confidence that the men and the principles that have
brought us to our present tragic pass will get us out of
it. The masses, meantime, hug to themselves the thorns
that are lacerating them. "We are uncomfortable," they
say, "so we will shift our position, or go a little faster in
the same direction; we will get out of one social class into
another, or we will swap one political party for another."

No isolated project, no spasm of reform or series of
such spasms, no mere revolution, no benevolence in our

leaders, will suffice in a situation like this. For it is a general human-nature situation. The human nature that is within us must turn critically upon itself, or we shall be lost. We shall be lost because, in the first place, the enormous forces that the sciences make available are of such kinds, and the habits and massed sentiments the world over are of such kinds, that conflict and destruction are in the air. They are not merely in the air; they are integral to the supposed wisdom of our leaders and to the uncritical assumptions of the led. We shall be lost because, in the second place, the impulses that have created the present conflict and destruction are permanent, not incidental and temporary. We have to wrestle with the project as a method of nature—nothing less than this.

The conclusion is, first, that an essential mark—nay, the most clearly distinguishing mark—of *educational* projects is the purposed and habitual inclusion within the activities of pupils as well as teachers of free criticism of human life and of human nature; second, that this free criticism, and the action necessary to give it effect, are functions of all persons, not merely of those who (through any cause whatever) may be in positions of special influence. Thus, the culmination of project method will be a continuous project in the never-ending democratic *re*-construction of life.

CHAPTER IV

NATURAL LAW AND TEACHER-LAW IN THE PROJECT

Probably no question connected with the project movement has created more difficulty than this: If the pupil is to be educated through his own purposeful acts, through decisions made and executed by himself, what is the function of the teacher? Does the project imply abnegation of control, or rather a more subtle way of "putting over" predetermined designs? Is the pupil to have real initiative and control, or is he merely to think so and be happy over it? The answer has to be sought in several directions. In a later chapter we shall see that much depends upon our conception of the most desirable social order, for example. But a part, an important part, of the answer grows directly out of natural laws that determine the changes that take place in children. The functions of the teacher are being settled for us by advances in our understanding of physiological and psychological facts. Here, at least, definite knowledge, rather than opinion or adherence to any contested social ideal, is decisive. The evidence for this proposition is near at hand.

It is a historical fact that the more we study children, even by unprecise methods, the more we trust their spontaneities. An experienced leader of boys said: "There may be bad boys, but I have never known one." Out of long experience in the junior department of the

Sunday school a trained leader and keen observer remarked: "I have never known a class of junior children to make a wrong decision after they really understood the case." When analysis of child life grows more precise, so does our confidence. We cease to think that we need to teach a child to walk; we slough off the superstition that small children must be kept amused; we learn that many child impulses that we used to regard as troublesome are really great educational assets; we are convinced that in the normal child there are at work likewise certain checks and balances that tend to keep activity wholesome and to promote rest and other recuperative processes. From all this the inference *appears* to be direct that wherever the capacities of normal pupils for initiative and self-guidance are utilized, there control by the teacher diminishes.

This inference is drawn from experience with normal children under normal conditions. Abnormality, whether congenital or merely incidental, seems to reverse the rule. A disturbance of digestion can put out of action the appetite for wholesome food; such a disturbance can likewise prevent the social reactions upon which the value of school contacts largely depends. Mouth-breathing lessens the capacity for responses to certain sorts of stimuli. Chronic irritation in a bodily organ may obstruct organized thinking, and so render continuity of purpose in a project difficult or impossible. But why heap up examples? Granted that the discovery and correction of such defects wherever possible are functions of the school; granted merely that teaching must adapt itself to such conditions, it follows that increased scientific acquaintance with the abnormal child enlarges the teacher's sphere of action and increases his control of the pupil.

Now, this experience with abnormalities has reacted in a remarkable manner upon our whole notion of normality and upon our handling of it. When scientifically guided schooling was first provided for delinquents and defectives, the remark was common that they were better looked after than normal children. Then, when medical examinations, school nurses, school dietetics, tests of intelligence, and special classes began to be accepted as normal parts of school administration, there was an awakening to the wide range of differences contained within the normal group. Gifted children were found to be suffering from educational neglect just as truly as children of retarded intelligence. Old methods of classifying pupils were found to be crude and even obstructive. Then, too, not all the important differences are comprised under the heads of physical health and native intelligence. Temperament, of which we shall probably learn something practical from the new studies of glandular secretions, is unquestionably a fundamentally determining factor in any child's educative experience. Even the cumulative effects of living in a given home environment, the ingrained "sets," necessitate differentiated treatment. Facts like these have made some persons skeptical of the whole custom of teaching children in masses. After all, is not the "normal child" an abstraction, practically a fiction, being merely the middle part of a measuring stick? As observation broadens and deepens, "the normal child" and even "the child" tend to fade from living thought.

The result of scientific analysis, then, is to extend the area of the teacher's control, and to refine it, with *both* normal and abnormal pupils. There is less of vagueness, guesswork, and generality when one starts a thing going, and there is closer scrutiny of results. The schoolmaster of yesterday, who deduced his method from educational dogmas, and then defended the product on the ground that it must be good because the dogmas were true, made a great show of control. He was strict; he could keep children quiet in their seats for hours at a time; he could make them define an improper fraction and recite fifty dates. But tnis was a relatively external control; it missed altogether a hundred areas, physiological and psychical, in which important reactions were occurring and important habits forming. Indeed, the degree of control that is achieved in abnormality becomes a standard and a guiding light for the education of children whose impulses are the healthiest, whose capacity for self-control is the greatest. Just as the dulness or refractoriness that nullified the teacher's plans before adenoids, tonsils, and diet were attended to gave way, after treatment, to active docility, so the pupil of superior capacity who was "bad" simply because he needed something to do became willingly obedient to school requirements when his load was regulated by scientific knowledge of his strength.

Thus, increased knowledge of normal children as well as abnormal has the following effects: We differentiate pupils from one another; we identify the particular need of each under particular conditions; we refine and differentiate the stimuli that we employ; our control, becoming more refined, covers also more points; and so, finally, the range and the depth of the control exercised by the teacher increase.

But notice, now, that this is the route whereby we achieve the project method. While this extension of the teacher's mastery has been going on, the pupil's freedom has been increasing. Not only does he feel fewer restraints and get along more comfortably, he actually initiates more of his own activities, and makes and executes decisions over a wider range of his conduct. Whether it is paradoxical or not, it is a fact that through one and the same process both the teacher's control of the pupil and the pupil's control of himself have increased.

This point is so important that an example or two, even from commonplace experience, may not be out of order. Let us take, first, a change in baseball games that was wrought through supervision of a certain playground. In the old days, when the boys were left to themselves, they were unable to organize the game so as to make it run smoothly. They did not know how to deal effectively with violation of rules, unfair playing, or deception. Such conduct, on the part of even one boy, could cause friction sufficient to break up a game. But with the coming of a supervisor the boys acquired—voluntarily and gladly—ability to handle such cases, and a settled habit and custom of doing so. The rules were better understood and better enforced; the satisfaction of contest and of conquest was increased, while chagrin at defeat was lessened, and withal the boys were proud of their heightened ability to control themselves.

A second example is the freeing of fettered wills by the teacher-controlled experience of learning how to study. Much of what was formerly called inattention, self-will, and obstinacy was really an obstructed will. And the teacher's will was obstructed at the same point until, through analysis of the thought process, he learned how to free both himself and his pupils.

It thus appears that when we are most faithful to the project principle, when we observe most strictly the conditions under which a pupil's energies become freely effective, we increase, not decrease the teacher's living authority. His decisions determine more of the pupil's activities, and the pupil consciously leans upon the teacher's wisdom more than before. Project method does not at all signify laissez faire.

This suggests that a fallacy has influenced much of our customary thinking concerning the relation between the teacher's authority and the pupil's freedom. The fallacy is that freedom or control or authority is a definite quantum, so that, in any social situation, if one member of the group possesses more the others have less. So bound are we, Bergson might say, to space-derived categories even when we endeavor to think the non-spatial. Freedom is like joy; sharing with my friend may double my own portion. We deal here not with a mechanical law, but with a spiritual law, that is, a law of relations between persons. A little later we shall see how the same law makes possible an increase of freedom through obedience to the social will. At the present moment, when our interest is in the significance of natural law for the project, we may tentatively formulate the principle as follows: *Mutual submission by teacher and pupil to conditions known by both to be imposed by natural laws tends to release the powers of both teacher and pupil, and thus tends to enfranchise both.*

This principle furnishes a corrective for two half-truths that are widely believed. The first is that the most educative experience is had through living one's present life, not by preparing for the future. The correction is that living one's present life upon the basis of natural law not only does prepare for the future, but does it consciously. One might argue this upon the entirely general ground that foresight and prearrangement of one's experience is of the inmost nature of rational human living. To be human is to be foresighted. What science does is to make prevision specific and accurate, and the more this is done the more free we are. To recognize causal relations in one's activities, as project method requires, is per se to prepare for future living.

The other half-truth is the current assertion that pupils learn most effectively when they do not think about the fact that they are learning. This dogma represents, not a law of the mind, but unfortunate conditions of learning that prevailed in the old-fashioned school. There, indeed, to be conscious that one was engaged in the learning process was to be reminded of the school or of the teacher or of schooling as something imposed upon one; it was to experience discomfort and an impulse to escape. In a situation like this there is undoubted gain when a pupil forgets the school, the teacher, and educational standards, and becomes absorbed in subject-matter. But the situation is profoundly reversed when school life means, not imposition by teacher and submission by pupil, but mutual submission to law, or fellowship in the scientific spirit. Pupils who are accustomed to witness the scientific approach everywhere in the school, constantly learning why this or that measure is taken with respect to heat, light, ventilation, dust, colds, food, body-weight, and much more, easily and happily learn to look forward, with the teacher, to gains in the learning process. As underweight children ambitiously drink milk (I heard one of them boast that he had drunk five glasses in one day), watch the scales and record their gains or losses in avoirdupois, so also interest arises in intellectual and social abilities, and in the processes whereby these abilities are increased. Then we see children imposing drill upon themselves, and keeping a record of their own progress. They do not feel that the teacher assigns marks to them, but that nature herself does. Under such conditions not only instinctive curiosity, and enjoyment in exercising one's powers are set free, but the natural desire to be a part of the world in which grown-ups live is indulged. It is indulged, not imitatively, or parrot-like, not by concealing the difficulties of growth, but by facing them and intelligently overcoming them.

When we clearly realize that through mutual submission to natural laws the teacher's control of pupils can be enlarged at the same time that their own freedom is increased, we may possibly pluck up courage to face the need of increased control of the young. There is truth in the frequently heard wail that the children of today are uncontrolled; lawless; lacking in respect for elders and for the past; lacking in reverence for the ideal and the holy; that they are subjected to too many exciting stimuli; that they are frittering away their powers upon worthless if not harmful pleasures; and that no sufficient barrier shields their minds from contamination from the sinful ways of adults.

The truth in this complaint is so great and so portentous that if there were in sight no better controls than those of the schools of yesterday (and, for the most part, of today), not only would this dejected wail be justified but settled pessimism also. The pre-project type of schooling fails to meet the need because it is weak precisely where the deleterious influences are strong, namely, in invitations to self-determination. Under the conditions of today most pupils who during school hours feel that they are subject to teacher-law pass, after school hours, into a world of apparent freedom. With this outside experience of apparent freedom school experience of the pre-project sort cannot successfully compete. It cannot do so either by compulsion, or by appeal, or by sugar-coated indirection—the pupil cannot unify the two worlds. Our only rational hope is that we may draw educative materials and processes directly from the stimuli that create the problem; that is, the school must enter, project-fashion, into the extra-school experiences of the pupil. It must face with him—that is, lead him to face, along with the teacher—the very situations that make the trouble. Now, the teacher's anxiety is based in part upon scientific foresight. He knows that this or that conduct will lead, under physiological or psychological laws, to an undesirable outcome. As a rule teachers do not fully share with pupils this scientific insight. The present suggestion is that projects (not preaching, but projects) directed toward securing whatever good the out-of-school environment has to offer, but guided by scientific insight into causes and effects—projects, that is, in which teacher and pupil alike submit to natural law—contain our only rational hope for a solution of the problem that confronts us.

This sort of approach to some community matters, as the use of libraries and museums, is already coming into vogue, and in a few instances the "movies" have been evaluated and improved. Why should not the pupil, with the teacher's help, travel thus the entire round of his environment in an endeavor to find "what there is in it for him"? Let him subject to real tests wholesome and unwholesome factors, and thus let teacher-law be transformed into something more persuasive, even clear foresight of natural-law consequences.

Some of the points at which increased control of children appears to be essential may be enumerated. The following list is not exhaustive, but it should be suggestive. A few of the items are included in this natural-law group because of the prominence of the natural law of habit-formation.

Habits of diet.
The soda fountain.
Habits of rest.
Cleanliness.
Sanitation.
The use of stimulants and of narcotics.
Plays and games.
Commercialized sports, and in general the sports of adults.
Frequency of attendance at moving-picture shows.
Safety of moving-picture houses. Sanitary and hygienic conditions therein.
Social conditions and influences incident to attendance at moving pictures.
Character of moving pictures presented in the community.

Billboard advertising.

The newspaper habit, with respect to discrimination of important news from unimportant, and with respect to the extent and the character of "comics," sporting news, and descriptions of vice and crime.

The acquisition, possession, and use of money by children and youth.

The habit of "going somewhere." Under this head I include not only the psychic effects of motoring as it is practiced, but also all the current methods of obtaining a rapid succession of sense stimuli. The amusement park belongs here.

Standards of dress and of personal adornment.

Habits and ideas connected with sex and the family.

Gambling, both by children and by adults.

The mutual submission of teacher and pupil to natural law helps to solve still other problems that concern the teacher's functions and authority. The following conditions have frequently to be met: First, because of the rapidity and inexorableness of natural law, the teacher is under obligation to decide some things in advance of all thinking and deciding by the pupil; second, for similar reasons, sometimes the teacher must vigorously take the initiative in a project, and yet lead students to make it their very own; third, a part of the scientific truth and a part of the teacher's purpose must sometimes be withheld from the pupil for a time. In the atmosphere of science all three of these can be done without weakening the project attitude and habit of the pupil.

How the matter works may be illustrated by children, counted as normal, who nevertheless need a new dietary habit or corrective muscular exercises. The number of such children is far greater than was dreamed of in the educational philosophy of yesterday; how great it is

will not be known until thorough pediatric and ortho-
pedic examinations are the rule rather than, as now,
the exception.

Let us take, first, the overactive, underweight, and
undersize child who tends toward nervousness. His
name is legion, and he is frequently found among those
whose IQ is high. He is not sick or deformed; he needs
neither medicine nor surgery; his is a case for education.
Therefore, he is led to compare his weight with a scale
of normal age-weights; the weight-producing foods are
explained, and he is led into the project of increasing
his weight. Nothing is said about his being undersize,
lest a sense of inferiority should arise. Next, on the
playground the supervisor, with the least possible show
of control, sees to it that this child, in any game that is
played, has one of the less strenuous parts. Yet it is
found experimentally that even very ambitious boys,
once they have adopted the project of increasing their
weight, will submit to rigorous prohibitions with every
appearance of conviction.

A similar attitude can be developed in children who
need exercises that will correct faults of posture and
carriage. The girl referred to in the first chapter
is an example. Her school is one in which, because
scientific care in such matters is an established and
fully understood part of the administration, the pupils
themselves get the spirit of it. The teachers, for their
part, say little about defects, but much about gains and
conquests, and as far as practicable they devise games
or contests of appropriate sorts instead of formal gym-
nastics. Hence we see the pupils, with jolly enthusiasm,
taking as their own the teacher's project-in-general;

we see this general project dividing and subdividing, every part having meaning for the pupils, but not necessarily the whole meaning that the teacher has in mind; and in every part we witness an intelligent leaning upon the wisdom of the physical director. This leaning deserves careful scrutiny. It is not subservience to authority in the fashion of the schools of yesterday; it is not blind attachment to an attractive personality; it is the acceptance of guidance by science recognized as such. It reaches its maximum when the pupils realize that the director himself is not subservient to a mere tradition or custom, but is studying, learning, and modifying his own procedures in response to increasing scientific insight.

When natural law, apprehended by scientific processes, becomes a pervasive factor in the school consciousness, a guide in the whole ongoing of the school and not merely something that is studied in classes in "science," it acts as a bond of union between the personalities involved, a bond between pupil and pupil, and between pupil and teacher. Then the whole school experience tends to assume the project character, and in the process, though what has been known as the teacher's "authority" wanes, his prevision and real control increase just as the pupil's prevision and real control also increase.

CHAPTER V

THE WILL OF THE PUPIL AND THE WILL OF SOCIETY

The project principle asserts that the educative process goes forward with the greatest power where the pupil forms and executes purposes of his very own. When, then, is one's will one's very own? Was the purpose of Jean Valjean his own, or that of his masters, when, a convict slave, his muscles strained at the oars of the galley? Was the purpose of Othello his own, or Iago's? When the Roman rabble, excited by Antony's speech, made up what it thought was its own mind, and proceeded to work what it thought was its own will, did it really work its own will or that of another? When an American citizen enters a polling booth and secretly marks a ballot as he will, how far does he himself determine how he shall mark it, and how far is he an instrument of a party or of a class in society? When a teacher, with canny forethought, places illustrated story books within the reach of young children, and reads samples of the stories to show what is inside the books, whose will really determines matters when the children, at their own request, are permitted to learn to read? When a history project, or a civics project eventuates in an enthusiastic conviction that ours is "the best government on earth," who does the real thinking in the case?

How much, then, do we really say, and what do we precisely mean, when we advocate education of the young through decisions that they themselves make and execute? Even when I am under compulsion my act may be in some sense my own, and when I am least restrained my decision may be less mine than that of surrounding persons. A part of the answer to this question has been given by Professor Kilpatrick in his analysis of the difference between choosing a painful thing because the alternative is still more painful, and choosing something that is not only relatively satisfying, but inherently so. The difference (educationally) is in the concomitant learning and in the mind-sets that are produced. A child who, being given the alternatives of learning the multiplication table or taking a whipping, decides in favor of arithmetic, and carries out his decision, may learn the multiplication table, but he is likely to learn likewise habits of evasion, and of overvaluation of appearances and of teachers' marks, and he is likely to acquire mind-sets against mathematics, the teacher, and even schooling as a whole. Obviously the concomitant learning and the mind-sets are likely to be far better when one encounters multiplication as an invitation to an inherently satisfying activity. Hence, the project principle certainly implies an intention on the teacher's part to avoid compulsion of pupils.

Yet compulsion of the individual by society is a fact that somehow must be faced. The parent is compelled to pay taxes, to obey the sanitary code, and to obtain a license before he runs a motor car. The teacher himself is compelled to do disagreeable things, such as making out reports. We know of no way to dispense with compulsion as one of the bonds that hold us adults together in society. And of course authorita-

tive command, both to do and not to do—reduce it as
much as we possibly can—must be held in reserve for
emergency use in the protection of children from evils
that they do not appreciate. What, then, does the
project principle imply at these points?

What does it mean, too, in the innumerable positive
matters that require of the teacher a degree of foresight
and of prearrangement of which his pupils are incapable?
How can one teach at all without selecting, in advance of
all pupil decisions, the general direction in which pupils
are to move, and in many instances even the specific
acts that an individual should be led, of his own volition,
to perform? A convenient example of such specific
acts is the use of a toothbrush. This is not compulsion,
but it is control. The pupils make their own decisions and
execute them, yet within these decisions there are operative prior decisions of society acting through the school.

Such situations in the school are not only not exceptional, they represent a general principle of social
psychology. The will of an individual never is and never
can be disengaged from the encompassing and permeat-
ing will of his fellows. The *mere* individual, it has been
remarked, is an abstraction. The evidence for this
paradox is found alike in the processes of the adult mind
and in the movement whereby, out of the selflessness of
the new-born, there emerges an individual self. This
evidence cannot here be given, but parts of it are easily
illustrated. It is easy to see that each of us tends to
reflect, even in innermost thought and feeling, the age
and the society in which he has his being. Even when
we have no intention of influencing another, and no
notion that we are being influenced, we do mutually form

one another's opinions, likes, dislikes, purposes, character. What sort of domestic architecture do you most like? Your reply, ten chances to one, reflects a current mass-liking expressed in the style of the time. The writer of these words recalls a whole procession of styles—of popular likes—from Mansard roofs and Queen Anne fronts through Dutch colonial, New England colonial, and German timbered stucco to the present hug-the-ground types. Why does the poetry of the Victorian era, that once seemed to us all-alive, now sound to us so like the hollowness of a dried seashell? Is it not that we have been carried along, without individual foresight, in a common current of life? Our political, moral, and religious attitudes and convictions, likewise, go in waves; they are principally mass movements. They represent periods, peoples, and minor groups. They are not, on the whole, aggregations of privately-arrived-at conclusions. Most of us for the most part simply "belong." Yes, science itself exhibits waves of mass interest, points of view, favorite problems and methods. The scientific man never is alone with the objects that he investigates, for "science" goes with him into field and laboratory. To our innermost core we are in and of groups, larger and smaller; in and of institutions and customs; in and of imitative or co-operative occupational, political, scientific, ethical, and religious thinking and doing. We grow up to be persons in no other manner. Not only does our early environment of persons give us many of our permanent sets; a baby achieves the human type of mind at all only by interplay with others of his species. Personality itself is a social fact.

We are faced by ambiguity, consequently, in the concept of the project. For what a pupil does, even when he is most individual and self-guided, is wrought *in* him as well as *by* him. It is wrought in him, first, by the immediate school environment. The school exists, not as his device, not even by his sufferance; and his presence there is determined by a joint willing. The will of the state, the will of his family, the sentiment of his social class, the standards of his prospective occupation—one or more of these work within him, whether or not he willingly co-operates with them. His fellow-pupils, too, are not of his selection; yet they enter intimately into his attitudes, decisions, and activities of every sort. The teachers are not appointed by him, and their policies antedate all his projects; yet the teachers, too, whatever their methods, participate in his inmost activity.

Moreover, teacher and pupil together are under constant pressure from out-of-school forces. Part of this pressure takes the form of school laws and ordinances and administrative policies. Trace the history of the selection of a site for a school, the laying-out of the grounds, the choice of an architect, the ideas that determine the plans of the building, the making of the budget, the levying of school taxes, the election of a superintendent, yes, the employment of a janitor—trace this through, with the pupils of the school in your mind's eye, and you shall see the social will entering into the pupil's will, now as a rising sun of aspiration, and now as the narrowing, the choking, the distortion of a personality. What, then, does this imply with respect to the project method?

The community acts within the teacher and the pupil not only thus by laws, ordinances, and official administration, but also in many subtler ways. A varied terminology bears witness to unofficial, often undefined and unrecognized, forces that work within our wills partly by reasoning, partly by persuasion, but still more by suggestion. Consider the fact back of each of these terms: public opinion; public sentiment; the spirit of a people or of a nation; the spirit of the times; national destiny; race destiny; class-consciousness; race-prejudice; up to date; respectability; success; "good fellow"; being in the game; "he-man"; "red-blooded"; "red"; "100 per cent American"; practical; common sense; humanity; "a square deal"; foreigner, ... but why prolong the list? Here are—not abstractions or speculative entities, but—living forces that circulate in the pupil's most individual feeling, thinking, and acting. They act as assumptions, or predeterminants, and they are all the more effective for this reason. They are effective, too, not only as determinants of this or that immediate product, but likewise in the deeply educative way of producing mind-sets, or channels within which one's energies shall hereafter flow.

The interlocking of such assumptions, too, is extensive and important, for it results in supporting one assumption by another. Consider, for example, the unexpressed social urge that surrounds and penetrates the child's mind with respect to the possession, the use, and the acquisition of money. Like the roots of a pine tree, this urge pushes far out in many directions, and far down. It controls to a large degree the child's notions and attitudes with respect to power—what one wants, and how to get it; labor; success; social classes; various personal habits; law and justice. These are not mere notions, let it be remembered, nor yet passing interests like fondness for a toy, but permanent impulsions from society that enter cumulatively into a large proportion of the pupil's real projects.

In every school project, then, society and the pupil jointly purpose and jointly produce whatever is produced —most of all the part of the product that remains as a permanent residuum. The project method does not at all get rid of the duality of factors that teachers have recognized and struggled about since the beginning of formal education. But a change in the relation of the two certainly occurs when we wholeheartedly adopt this method. What is this change? Is it an alteration in pupils' attitudes and procedures, the social or extra-school factor remaining the same, or do both factors undergo complementary modifications? Certainly the teacher who makes the shift undergoes a marked transformation, not least at the points where he most precisely represents the authority of society, as in discipline. Between pupil and teacher, at least, a new type of joint willing is born. What we need to know, accordingly, is whether the changed policy on the teacher's part is merely a new tool for bringing the pupil into accord with the same old social forces. Is the project merely a subtler mode of conforming the pupil to a predetermined social model, or is the new method, as to the pupil it appears to be, a sincere, uncamouflaged presentation of social reality?

Probably the very first point at which an answer to this question should be had is the relation of the secondary school to the elementary school, and the second, the relation of the college to the secondary school. If life in its reality is sincerely presented to children in elementary projects—the *method* of living together and learning together, on the one hand, and what to live *for*, on the other—then what should be the significance for him and for society of his entrance into the secondary school? When I witness the vitality, the social reality, and the perspective of various school projects of young children, and then see high-school pupils poring for hours every evening over assigned lessons, not because they are in themselves important, but because one's standing in class is at stake, I cannot repress a feeling of injustice. "What studies do you have?" I asked of a high-school pupil. The various subjects were named. Picking out one of them, I said, "Why do you study it?" "Because it's required for graduation in my course," was the reply. "But why is it required?" I persisted. "I do not know!" said the victim. The high-school pupil is likely to be loyal to such tasks, yes; and such devotion never goes altogether unrewarded. Nevertheless, moving up from the grades into the high school should not mean a narrower freedom, a narrower co-operation, a contracted measure for life's values. Already there is felt in our best elementary schools the embarrassment of a duality of principles in the educational system. Similarly, the secondary schools that deal most vitally with the life of the community have long felt that the movement of the student toward and into the college is a movement toward and into the relatively abstract.

This is not the place to discuss the function of the high school in the community, nor yet the overwhelming problem of the general purposelessness that pervades the colleges, but one may venture the assertion that there is nothing greater in the kingdom of education today than children who confidingly take project teaching at its face value as representing real life. The sincerity of society in its encouragement of this attitude will be proved at some cost, however, and first of all in the reconstruction of secondary and higher education.

Our discussion has brought us within sight of three points that concern the relation of the project to the pupil's will, on the one hand, and to the will of society, on the other. First, within school projects there remains, and always must remain, a factor of compulsion. Second, even within the most completely voluntary activities of pupils in their school projects, society still exercises broad control; it wills *within* the pupil's willing. Third, this joint willing, which is of the essence of the project, implies (if we value sincerity) a two-sided, not merely a one-sided, plasticity. As the pupil finds his way by the help of the social will as expressed in school organization and method, so society finds its way by the help of the pupil's experience as he knows and judges it in his projects. Thus, at one and the same point the pupil and society make experiments in living; both submit their case to the test of a changing and enlarging experience that is mutually initiated and mutually judged.

We have come within sight of this third point, but the evidence for it thus far is drawn from the presumption that the school, as an organ of society, is sincere when it invites the pupil to find what is true and good through his own voluntary activities. We need not rest the case here, however. One can safely venture the assertion that the teachers who have consistently pursued the project method have themselves learned something thereby as to how to live, and especially how to live together. Certainly, this is the drift of what one hears. It is rather fascinating, in fact, as it surely is new, to hear teachers boasting that they are learning at least as much as their pupils. Again, times uncounted pupils' projects have been a tonic for the will of the community, of public officials, and of parents. Farming has been improved; so has housekeeping; sanitation and hygiene have been extended; fire hazards have been lessened; parks and playgrounds have been provided; immigrants have been induced to become citizens—all because fresh young minds, with time for thinking, and unhampered by conventionalities, went straight toward some of the simple essentials of living, and their elders took them seriously.

What will happen when other fresh young minds, for a generation or two, proceed to get acquainted with a hundred other adult ways of doing things? One does not dream wildly who foresees many a social change coming to pass because the eyes of children peer into our police stations, our jails and prisons, courts, charitable and correctional institutions, taxation and budgets, industrial conditions, welfare legislation, even international relations. When Jesus said that in order to enter into the greatest things in life one must become as a little child, he uttered a truth so greatly simple that it required generations and generations for men to begin to see the sweep of its meaning. It is literally true that adults go on century after century inflicting upon themselves and their offspring losses and hurts and injustices that could be avoided by adding the simple wisdom of children to that of parents and teachers.

The churches will get better acquainted with their Master when they heed his words about children. Not long ago some Sunday-school pupils were led into the project of participating with the congregation in the Sunday-morning worship. Worship was studied and planned for, and the children entered the sanctuary ready to make reverent response to everything, from the first note of the organ voluntary. But adults whispered during the voluntary, and people came in late, to the distress of the children. When the fact that their worship had been thus interfered with was communicated to the church society, a reform of adult practices was inaugurated. Just so, who can measure the new energies of many sorts that will flow through the churches when "a little child shall lead them"? What dropping of cumbersome paraphernalia! What emancipation from institutionalism! What simplification of purpose, and what directness and wholeheartedness of aim! What unification of forces that are now divided over purely adult differences! The project in religious education—the project as a mutually sincere joint willing on the part of children and adults— may well prove to be the means of salvation for the churches.

Co-operative willing, then, is of the essence of the project, and co-operative willing implies renunciation of arbitrariness on all sides. This conception vacates the criticism that the project principle, implying reduction of the "Thou shalts" and "Thou shalt nots," must result in individual self-seeking. We should violate the principle itself if, mistaking the nature of individuality, we encouraged any child to think that he can have *his own* way by anything short of co-operation. To take the individualistic road is not to achieve independence of thought or of choice, but only a different set of dependences—usually dependence upon a careless, reckless, partisan, or (as often occurs) a tyrannical group opinion, and slavery to the purveyors of selfish satisfactions.

Now, the only known guaranty against the development of arbitrariness is experience of the co-operative spirit in other persons. Compulsion may wear out this or that impulse, and at such a point it may produce passive conformity, to be sure, but whatever of self remains is still untrained. Is any sort of arbitrariness more disagreeable than that of a thoroughly institutionalized mind? Criticism of the method of pupil freedom from the standpoint of the school of yesterday, therefore, is pecularly malapropos. It is amazing, in fact, that teachers ever imagined that arbitrariness and self-seeking are best prevented by what, to the pupil's experience, seems to be an exercise of arbitrariness on the part of others.

We need to dig deeper than we usually do about the two difficulties that seem to call for exceptions to the project principle. In the first place, the danger of arbitrary, self-seeking, or partisan use of freedom by the pupil cannot be met by a policy of abridging his freedom, but only by a policy of increasing his freedom by extending the range of his self-expression through co-operation. We teachers need, too, to be more objective in our thinking concerning our competence, and the competence of adult society, to assume the rôle of infallible guide. Who that contemplates the condition of humanity all over the world today can fail to see that our traditional assumption of authority over children in the interest of adult standards and adult ways of doing things needs revision?[1] In the second place, we should not hastily assume that the necessity of compulsion by society involves exceptions to the project principle. We should rather explore a little farther the implications of the necessarily social nature of individuality itself. It will appear, I think, that what is called for is not exceptions but a thorough carrying-out of the project process itself as genuine, two-sided, co-operative thinking and willing, with all the reciprocal judgments, on both sides, to which this leads.

Let us see whither this principle will lead us. It will certainly require us to give the same kind of respect to the personality of a child that we give to that of a grown-up. Not indulgence, or coddling, or concealment of reality; not the building-up of a separate child-world that will later meet disillusionment; not two contradictory modes of social organization—democracy for adults and sugar-coated autocracy for children—but the very same processes (graded, of course, to children's growing capacity) of social recognition, mutual adjustment, and mutual control. This implies that, just as society, acting through the teacher, exercises rights of selection that the pupils may not override, so the pupils, on their side, have rights of selection that society, acting through the school, may not abridge. It implies, likewise, that, as the judgment of society, expressed through the teacher, approves and condemns processes and products, and requires revisions, so, likewise, the pupils

[1] Cf. p. 39.

approve and condemn society as it is, call for revisions, and have effective ways of making their judgment upon society count. Is not this, indeed, just what has happened repeatedly where the project method has brought pupil will and social will face to face, as in matters of sanitation and parks and playgrounds?

If we do thus include in the concept of the project a full realization that "real-life situations" educate in living better than miniature, or invented, or merely symbolical situations, we shall in the end commit ourselves to the principle that children should participate in the control of society in the large in the same sense and by the same methods (though not to the same degree) as adults. If in the project the choosing and executing are genuinely reciprocal as between the pupil and society (as represented by the school), then neither party may claim any complete exemption from the judgment of the other. Both parties must possess authority in the same sense.

The ways in which social control is wielded are various. One of them is "talking matters over." Many a teacher learned this long before "project" had a place in the technical terminology of teaching. What is now necessary is to be ready and willing to change sides in such "talking over." We must make it easy and natural for pupils, of their own initiative, to say what they find satisfactory and unsatisfactory in the school, in the home, in the church, and in society at large. "Talk it over" with the teacher, the principal, the superintendent, the school board. It ought to be a natural and expected occurrence for school children to take their judgments before the board of education. What reciprocal illumination would result, and what increased and improved purposefulness all around.

Let us consider for a moment how unnatural and wasteful our present situation is in this respect. From the old, repressive theory of training we have inherited the almost universal, but deadening, opinion that schools and schooling as such cannot be vitally willed by pupils. It is high time to recognize the evil lineage of this notion, and likewise to see the implications of the rapidly amassing instances of self-schooling, even in such difficult matters as formal drill. Here—to touch upon another type—is a boy who, in order to overcome a habit of "crabbing" or "knocking," willingly keeps upon his person a device for reminding himself and recording his slips. Other children, learning of the project, came to the teacher to ask for similar devices to help them overcome other social faults in themselves. It is astonishing how little use schools have made of children's aspiration to grow up. Astonishing, too, is our slowness to perceive how often the very simplicity and unconventionality of the child's mind enables it to go straight to the heart of large problems. When pupils once get into the way of easily and comfortably "talking it over" with school authorities, not only will schools become a mutual project of children and adults, but indefinite improvement will follow. Why, indeed, should not pupils have some part in staff meetings? What a satire upon our education in and for democracy is the college faculty meeting in which the students, many of them possessing the franchise of the state, have no part or lot!

This principle applies to all the relations of pupil to society. "Talk it over" with the policeman, the chief of police, the police judge, your alderman, your mayor, your representatives in legislature and congress, your governor, your president. None of them can get into "the kingdom" of good, responsible government until they become as little children. "Talk it over" with parents, Sunday-school teacher, superintendent, pastor. They, too, have no other road into the kingdom of the spirit.

Another method of social control is publicity. That evils thrive so much better in the dark than in the light is complimentary to human nature. Often all that is necessary in order to secure appropriate action is to get a fact before people's minds, and hold it there. But here a distinction is necessary. We have fallen upon a time when making public opinion is a technical manufacturing process as truly as making a chair. Governments, political parties, economic groups, and advertisers vie with one another in the use of psychological laws in such a way as to do people's thinking for them when they suppose that they are doing their own thinking. This is propaganda in an evil sense; it is fundamentally undemocratic, and in the end it becomes immoral. Entirely different is the employment of scientific method in the ascertainment of fact, and publicity for both fact and method. Participation of pupils in publicity work of this sort has already yielded splendid results, as in sanitation. Now, what pupils have done in the matter of flies as disease carriers points the way to other public service. Let them once form the habit of making public any facts whatsoever that they regard as socially important—facts concerning the school, public health, charities, government, industry, living conditions, morals, religion—and we shall have better schools and better community living as a result. And not merely facts that reveal defects. Understanding the community's strong points, and reasonable pride in them, is indispensable to sound social judgment and to the correction of faults.

Is there, indeed, any sort of social control that ought to be completely withheld from school children? No; the road upon which the project principle has started us will lead at last to pupil participation in government in the sense of political rights the same in kind, though not in degree, as those possessed by their parents and teachers. At present, though our political philosophy declares that there is no just government without the consent of the governed, all minors are ruled without their consent, even in matters that are universally recognized as within their capacity. *Degrees of capacity to govern* are utterly unrecognized in our constitutional law. In a single instant, when the hands of the clock touch the midnight hour, our young people pass from zero right of franchise to maximum right.

The scheme is almost incredibly crude. It is in no wise geared into our educational system. The state trains its children for citizenship for eight years in the elementary school, then for four years in the high school, and often for four years more in the college—*trains them for citizenship*—yet at no point in the process does the state satisfy itself, or certify to pupil or parent, whether or not any degree of competence as a citizen has been achieved. Graduation from the course of study prescribed by the state is not graduation into any function or right of the citizen whatsoever. Yet we wonder why adolescents show so little sense of social responsibility, so little respect for law, and why educated Americans do not feel the weighty import of the ballot!

Many an effort to fill this gap has been made, it is true. Witness the various schemes of so-called self-government, especially those that imitate the municipal, the state, or the national structure. That valuable social experience has been had through these and other modes of pupil control, no one will question. But they are inadequate. Most persons who think about the problem at all would agree, without doubt, that the only really good school government is that in which the pupils themselves achieve reflective, social self-control, and that training *for* democracy must be, in the nature of the case, training *in* democracy. Yet, under our present laws, every scheme of pupil self-government is inevitably infected with a certain untruth. For pupils have no right to self-government; they are merely permitted to run their own affairs by a teacher, a principal, or a superintendent who, as far as pupil self-government is concerned, is an irresponsible ruler. His whim may inaugurate it, or keep it out altogether; may determine its specific form; may nullify its acts, or abolish it without redress. A shift in the school staff may dislocate a whole social system in the school. Under such conditions the pupils, whatever the form of school government, do not get an experience of citizenship, but of an imitated, more or less artificial, substitute for it. Such substitutes, let me repeat, have undoubted value. To "get the hang" of holding meetings, electing officers and holding office, serving on committees, and thinking in group terms is not a small matter. But the citizen's experience of being the source of law at the same time that he is subject to it, the experience of wielding a share of genuine sovereignty, is lacking. The pupils know this, of course. To them, citizenship is off yonder as yet; it will arrive of itself when the clock strikes the hour; meantime their self-government is poised in unstable equilibrium between reality and make-believe.

What will the project principle do with a situation like this? It certainly will not give a dogmatic answer, nor offer a cut-and-dried program of reconstruction. But it surely will move forward, by cautious experimentation, in the direction of its own plain implications. First, the capacities of children for governing will be determined and graded by projects that place the maximum rather than the minimum of discretion in their hands in "real-life situations." Second, teachers and pupils together will then, by "talking it over" and publicity, show the school board and the voters (or, in the case of the church, the church board and the church members) the meaning and the advantages of incorporating pupil self-government (or, better, school self-government, for the teacher will always be included in vital projects in this field) into the official regulations of the board. Then, for the first time, the teacher, principal, and superintendent will abnegate their prerogative of arbitrariness, and for the first time the project method will become the method of a school board. Third, further experiment, on this new level, doubtless with many a miss as well as some hits, will lead finally to the project of incorporating the scheme into the statutes of the state and at last into the constitution too.

Some apparently essential features of such real self-government are as follows: First, it will be, not an optional privilege (a right without a duty), but, in broad outline, a legal obligation upon both teacher and pupil. Second, wide discretion and room for local adaptation will be guarded, but machinery for enforcement will be provided (a new type of juvenile court being included), so that dereliction by either teacher or pupil can be corrected at the instigation of anyone inside the school or outside it. Third, filling one's place successfully at any grade will lead to promotion to more rights and responsibilities, and at a definite point the successful self-governor will graduate into the full franchise of the state.

Early in this chapter the question was asked, At points where compulsion of the pupil is necessary, what does the project principle signify? We now have the answer: Place the necessary compulsion in a system in which everyone both exercises compulsion upon everyone and submits to compulsion from everyone, and let the particular experience be seen in its relation to the whole. You then have the conditions of a possible loyalty to what is disagreeable, a possible project that plainly and openly includes being compelled.

CHAPTER VI

HOW THE YOUNG ASSIMILATE MORAL LAW

In the last chapter we reached the conclusion that social education, if it is to be well-rounded, must include —not merely as a goal, but also as a living part of the educative process—the experience of governing as well as of being governed, "governing" being here used in the full sense of political society. This brings us to the related problem, not less delicate and difficult, of the relation of moral law, the "oughts and ought nots," to the freedom and vitality of the project. Is the pupil to be merely subjected to certain moral laws which the school authorities formulate, or is he to have a part in the creation of moral standards themselves? Is moral evolution to go forward in and through the project experience of the young, and if so, by what methods of teaching? These problems require the discussion of three questions, namely:

I. How does moral law become a control in the conduct and the projects of the young? The question is not, What control ought moral law to have? nor yet, What steps shall we take to give it increased control? but, What is the actual mechanism of control?

II. What is the relation of this process, now occurring in the young, to the process of moral transmission and moral evolution in society at large? In particular, what is the actual relation of the school to society in respect to morals?

III. What light do the answers to I and II cast upon the problem of method in moral education?

The first of these questions will be discussed in the present chapter, the remaining two in the chapter that is to follow.

I

1. The young encounter moral law, first of all, in the customs, or settled modes of action, of some group—a family, a play-group, children's parties, a school, a church, a city, a business community, and so on. The way in which anything is regularly or statedly done without protest in any group with which a child is associated is assumed to be the way this thing ought to be done. The remark is often heard that small children are ritualists, and innumerable tales are told of how they scrupulously reproduce in themselves, in their dolls, and if possible in their pet animals, some precise act that to them represents social reality. A pathetic phase of this process, often revealed when children play being father or mother, is the acceptance of parental arbitrariness and even cruelty as the to-be-expected, and therefore proper, conduct of a parent.

The psychology of this response to groups leads us into some of the profoundest aspects of child experience. The small child's problem (not analyzed by himself, of course) is to obtain some definite, reliable points of reference—items that "stay put"—in a mass of experiences that are so largely strange to him, and so uncontrollable. Only as he discovers things that meet expectations can he be a self or have a meaningful world. His name is such a fixed phase of himself; so are the ways of doing things that are already habitual with him; in this small, familiar area he can feel himself as himself. So he clings to these things as matters of what we call the merest justice. Just so, that which can be relied upon in others; that which brings a sense of familiarity at each meeting with a person, hence repetition, is what makes his social world at all manageable in thought, or feeling, or conduct. If, when I retell a familiar story, I change a single word, I must be corrected—the story "ought" to be told just so. "Oughts and ought nots" like this, expressive of insistent expectation, are means whereby the child has any articulate world at all. Added to this are the instinctive social satisfactions that accompany the fulfilment of social expectations, likewise the satisfaction of making things happen according to expectation. The whole process gives rise to an imperative feeling that the established social way is the "right" way, and that this or that "ought" or "ought not" to be done.

We by no means outgrow this mental procedure when we leave childhood behind. Adults also approve and condemn—*morally* approve and condemn—upon the basis of familiarity and non-familiarity. If all the women we had ever known had always kept their faces veiled in the presence of men other than their husbands, the sight of an unveiled female face would give the same moral shock that it used to give the Turks. Many persons gave an ethical shudder when our women began to wear ankle-high skirts, but the shock, with its moral quality, faded away when such costumes became familiar sights. The way in which we are even beginning to take "knickers" for granted as an appropriate costume for women reminds me of a conversation in which, about twenty-five years ago, when women were riding bicycles, a professor of theology confided to me his conviction that the modesty of women was on the decline —otherwise, how could they bear to wear bloomers!

If each of us should make a catalogue of his own habitual moral approvals and condemnations, and then check those that obviously rest chiefly upon habitual expectation (or, in some instances, mere mode of defining), most of us would be surprised, and many of us would be less cock-sure than we are concerning the depth of our morality. Such a catalogue might well begin with the proper relations of the female in the family and in society at large, for this is an area in which we are waking up and making fresh moral discriminations. We might then go on to consider our convictions as to the moral inferiority of peoples unfamiliar to us. Perhaps important moral differences between peoples do exist, but we do not wait for the proof of it, for we judge upon the basis of unfamiliarity. Just so, the ethics of an occupation represent chiefly the way in which it actually is carried on. "What's wrong with it? We've *always* done it." As far as I have been able to ascertain, no church ever tries a minister for heresy because he teaches an outworn doctrine; the heretic, the wrongdoer, is always the one who says the unexpected or unconventional thing.

The point now to be noted is that, in the child's consciousness, whatever is conventional tends to be taken as the "right" and the "ought-to-be." Now, this is moral experience—not the whole of it, of course, but— genuine moral experience, not a mere accompaniment or adjunct thereof. We deceive ourselves and misunderstand children if we assume the contrary.

2. The second point at which children encounter and assimilate moral law is approvals and disapprovals of conduct, to which in many cases there are added rewards and especially punishments. Every child has much experience of being approved and disapproved; moreover, everyone lives constantly in the presence of judgments upon others. Apparently children have a peculiarly deep interest in penalties, whether at home, in the school, in the state's prison, or in fairyland. To be on the safe side one's self describes a part of the interest here, but beyond this is a spontaneous liking for the law-and-penalty category for both thought and imagination. I once invented a story that appeared to be the tale of a deep crime, but at the crucial point, where the supposedly guilty party was apparently to be exposed, I turned the tragedy into a joke by accounting for the whole action on the basis of a misunderstanding of a trivial circumstance. A twelve-year-old lad who had become absorbed in the story turned on me almost savagely and insisted that I give a different ending to it; somebody, he said, ought to be punished. He saw the point of the joke clearly enough, but his imagination was living among relations that adults count as ethical.

Exceedingly broad is the area of approvals and disapprovals of which children are witnesses, and deep is the effect. Whatever the social judgment that prevails in a child's environment approves or condemns may become an item in his moral consciousness. Thus he acquires moral attitudes toward individuals, parties and classes, institutions, policies, acts, motives, types of character. His thinking labels each of them with one or other of the two ethical tags in his possession, good and bad.   He may not reason why at all, and when he does reason he is most likely to reproduce items of adult talk that he has happened to hear.   So seriously, so morally, does he take his actual social environment.   It is scarcely necessary to ask whether, in this matter, his moral life is markedly different, as respects the process, from that of adults.

3. Since most children have contacts with more than one group, each of which serves as a moral authority, children's moral judgments are really groups or sets of judgments that may or may not be coherent with one another.   There is considerable evidence not only that these sets of judgments, or codes. commonly conflict with one another, but also that they have different degrees of reality for the children who hold them.   A gang or clique standard, for example, is likely to have the force of reality for one's self, while family standards, although sincerely assented to, seem to belong more in the world of father and mother, and Sunday-school standards in the realm of teacher and minister.   Thus we find, side by side, principles in active use, and principles in cold storage, so to speak.   We greatly need information as to the actual moral judgments of children, and as to whether they are functioning judgments or cold-storage judgments.   One would like to know, for example, whether many ten-year-old boys, brought up in middle-class families, are like this picture:

Of course, mother and dad are all right, and brother and sister. You mustn't say anything against them, especially mother.   I'll stick by all of them, of course. . . . . Of course mother and dad want me to be good, and they think I'm better than I really am. But it's easy for them to be good, and some day, when I'm grown

up, I'll be like them. . . . . What they tell you in Sunday school
is all right, too, only . . . . well, when I'm as old as my teacher,
maybe I'll be like her. . . . . Of course, I don't have to be as
good as ministers. . . . . As for school, of course what the teacher
and the books say is so; leastways it was so for Washington, and
Lincoln, and Thomas Edison. But she doesn't play marbles, or
foot-ball, and she doesn't belong to the gang that meets in our
barn. I s'pose she and Washington wouldn't fib or swipe things,
and they wouldn't say "gosh," and they wouldn't throw stones
at Curly Jim's gang, but then, ... well, some day I s'pose
I wont myself. . . . . But, O boy! wouldn't I like to be Babe
Ruth! . . . . And if I had a million dollars I'd buy two automobiles, and an aeroplane, and a dirigible. . . . . Yes, of course
I ought to get my lessons, but gee! all the boys'll be at the swimming hole, and I mustn't miss it. . . . . Am I a good little boy?
Naw, but I'm a good sport, and I don't snitch, and . . . . and
. . . . I'll stand by ma and dad.

When children make this distinction between the
principles they assent to and the principles they live by,
are they so very different from us adults? When we
ourselves speak of moral law, do we mean what we think
ought to be taken as such law, or rather the working
standards of our actual conduct? How do we determine
what is reasonable and practicable in the particular
circumstances in which we are placed?

Yes, I ought to love my competitor as myself, but business is
business. I have to conform to business customs or shut up shop.
Some day, perhaps, the way of doing business will be
changed. . . . .

Yes, in a really brotherly industrial order profits would not
come first and the good of the working man's children last, but you
see, when I sell the product of my factory I have to meet the
prices of my competitors. I am doing the best I can under the
circumstances. . . . .

Of course, in strictness I ought to do a full day's work for a full day's pay, but there's unfairness in the wage-and-profits system anyhow, and I'm not going to strain myself to increase the profits of those who already have more than they know what to do with. . . . .

Of course, the single standard of sex-morality is right, but as long as the sex-desire remains so strong you can't expect men to be too strict. Besides, I'm as good as the general run of them. . . . .

No, I'm not as good as I ought to be; I have faults, just as everybody has. I guess I'm just about a decent, average sort of fellow. Anyhow, my standing with my neighbors is O.K.

Thus do adults, just like children, distinguish between the theoretical "ought" and the practical, working rules by which self-judgment is actually guided. Moral laws are "accepted" that do not come home to us. Which ones do come home? As a rule, those that express the actual social situations with which we are most familiar, and especially the ones in which our purposes have free scope.

4. Yet, with children, as with adults, the disparity between the acknowledged standard and the working rules of one's social groups comes now and then to clear consciousness in the form of inner conflict. A sermon or a religious revival; an emergency of the nation; a poem or a story; a crisis in life, such as a great loss, a great peril, or romantic love; acquaintance with a strong or beautiful character; the hush of a sacrament; aesthetic elevation in the presence of natural beauty or through great music; the musings of adolescence; the direct appeal of a teacher—incidents like these now and again warm up cold and disused ideals, producing according to circumstances self-condemnation,

punctilious effort to raise conduct above the conventional level, zeal for reform, or a passion for the "right as such." Doubtless adolescents are, on the whole, more susceptible to this than either children or mature persons, but in all probability we underestimate rather than overestimate the capacity of childhood for such sentiments.

When they are aroused, how do they relate the individual to society? As a rule they simply bring some already professed social ideal out of cold storage. We take up the slack, so to say, in respect to fair play, kindliness, charitable deeds, promptness, honesty, our moods and tempers, or going to church and saying our prayers. That is, the general social outlines remain the same as before, but we improve the quality or amount of the filling. For example, a school child who is thus awakened may apply himself more industriously to his studies, though what it is to study and what the meaning of school is remain unchanged for him. Or, he may desist from evading the payment of his fare on the street car, yet never question the property right held by the company in the form of a perpetual franchise in the streets. Honor in business, utter squareness, are without question admirable ideals, but they do not ordinarily affect the prior question of the fairness or humanity of the structure of business itself.

I submit these four points as a fair account of the usual process whereby moral law becomes a control of the young. Nearly all the facts will be found to fall under these heads. Yet not quite all. Children do not *merely* accept law from their social environment; they are by no means doomed to the unending rebirths of a self-identical social authority. They can and they do participate in experiences in which social authority is re-created. In order to see that this is so, and how it comes about, we need only consider the relation of children to each of the three fundamental concepts of ethics, "ought—ought not," "right—wrong," and "good —bad." Though "good—bad" is probably the most used ethical term of childhood, the corresponding concept is used less than the other two. The good and the bad are not ordinarily understood by children as referring to desirable or undesirable end-results of human situations produced by an act or expressed in it. Rather, the child thinks of superposed pains and penalties, or occasionally rewards, together with the corresponding social classification, and approval or disapproval, of the agent or of his act. A "good" child is traditionally one who is compliant toward his elders. That is, for the most part "good" is anything that is approved, and "bad" anything that is condemned, by adults. This, I say, is the usual state of the child mind. But it is not the invariable state, and it may be made by education less usual than it is.

For even children press back to the sources of ethical impulse, thinking no longer of a law to which one submits, but of some self-evidencing good or self-evidencing bad as a possible end-result of conduct. A delightful story is told of a child who was restless at night because he kept thinking how he would like to put a drop of cold water on Dives' tongue! A pupil in a primary class in a Sunday school, after hearing the story of the passage of the Israelites through the Red Sea, was invited to look at a Tissot picture of it. "Mrs. M.," said she to the teacher, "it doesn't seem fair that the horses, too, should be drowned." A boy of about six asked: "Were any children drowned in the Flood—any very little children that didn't know how to do right?" What has been called children's sense of justice has been noticed by everybody who studies children. It is often an echo of adult standards—sometimes a cruel echo, as in children's almost universal belief in the justice of savage punishments. Yet now and then, direct contemplation of a situation, say, of a persecuted dog, or of the amiable qualities of a member of the "lower classes," or of the grotesqueness of someone's moral self-conceit, or of the inefficiency of some standard process, produces an original moral valuation that outruns our moral conventionalities.

That adolescence, when it is not already withered by the desert heat of our competitive and selfish ways, or carried off its feet by the rush of modern life, is richly capable of these fresh appreciations, every student of the period has recognized. The ability of youth to take a fresh look, to sympathize, to dream, to aspire, to doubt, to be hotly for and hotly against the whole world, to believe that the desirable is practicable—all this constitutes one of the great moral assets of a progressive race. For it is in and through first-hand, unauthorized, not conventionally encouraged gazing into good and bad that conventional "ought—ought not," and "right—wrong," are judged and revised. The judging and revising have to become a group process, of course, but the start and the stimulus therefor originate in individuals who vary from the herd or from the institution.

Children and youth, then, can and do have a part in the renewal and reconstruction of moral law through contemplation of self-evidencing good. How large a part they might have, nay, how much we adults need their help, will not be known until we submit to their scrutiny various phases of our conduct that we now conceal from them. Writers of novels and of plays have not failed to perceive the dramatic possibilities in a situation in which an objective-minded young person, reared conventionally, for the first time perceives the human realities within, say, one's father's business. If, in our moral education, we should pursue the policy of leading children to observe and independently judge the actual facts of human weal and woe, who can doubt that our moral standards would rise with unprecedented rapidity?

Here, as so many times before, we come upon the parallelism—rather, the identity—of the moral experience of child and adult. Morality, as it was before our Civil War, required obedience to the fugitive slave law, but what was one to do when a human being, fleeing from servitude, came to one for help in reaching Canada? In spite of the wrenching of an old conscience, in spite of the birth-pang of a new conscience, many a northern citizen became a part of the "underground railroad," simply because it was the obvious, self-evidencing good. So the prophet of old, seeing the poor sold for a pair of shoes, beholding the great, landed proprietors panting even for the dust on the head of the poor, and realistically noting that the priesthood and the elaborate ceremonial worship at Beth-el were a support for the existing social system, boldly reinterpreted even God, declaring the Yahweh hated the sacrifices that were offered him; he desired only that justice should roll down as waters, and righteousness as a mighty stream.

Unless we think of the moral experience of men generally, the moral experience of children included, as capable of having a part in such re-creation of moral law—or, if one prefer, such fresh discovery of eternal moral law—we shall be as men who know the summer, autumn, and winter, of the arbutus, but not its spring.

CHAPTER VII

MORAL LAW AND MORAL CREATIVITY
IN THE SCHOOL

Having seen how moral law gets control of the young, we are ready to ask our second question:

II

What is the relation of this process, now occurring in the young, to the process of moral transmission and moral evolution in society at large? In particular, what is the actual relation of the school to society in respect to morals?

The answer has been given, in part, in the preceding chapter, where we saw children and adults acting alike. Obviously the moral process in the child is a miniature of the process in the race—rather, the two are continuous with each other. Moral evolution is going on in the experience of the young, and it might go on much faster.

Failure to perceive this truth, and to give it due weight in the theory of moral education, is the most deadly of all faults in current views of the school and its functions. For these views recognize only certain fractions of the moral experience, and the relation of child experience to moral evolution is ignored.

The fraction of the truth that is everywhere appreciated is that moral life in the young requires adjustment of an individual to an already existing social order. This adjustment takes the form, now of obedience to a rule even before it is fully understood, now of co-operation with those who are recognized as wiser, now as carrying one's load in the industrial system. Often a second fraction is recognized, namely, that moral law demands sympathy for distress, and respect for persons as such regardless of nationality and social class. What remains unrecognized, and of course unacted upon, may now be stated, along with comments upon the resulting gaps in current moral education.

1. The extreme readiness of the young to take the impress of the social order just as it exists, though this readiness contains one essential condition for the growth of moral character, makes the young the main vehicle for perpetuating the defects as well as the virtues of any age. The defective conventions, the prejudices, the evasions, practiced by existing society are transmitted within the moral experience itself, not merely by some extraneous and hostile process. Formulated principles, codes, public opinion, and institutions are obviously essential to social stability in the sense of the maintenance of the gains of past moral evolution; nevertheless they one and all represent the period of their origin; one and all tend to place together, and to make binding, moral relations into which the period of their origin was growing and those out of which it was moving. Thus all our funded morality becomes a bulwark not only of the good, but also of the not-good-enough. In other words, liability to ethical illusion inheres in morality as such, both in the race at large and in the experience of children. But no scheme of moral education appears to have grappled with the resulting problem. Teachers everywhere appear to assume that *moral process* in the

school is enough; no responsibility is taken for *moral evolution*.

2. A second capital fact of our social inheritance in the moral sphere is that one and the same process transmits both moral standards and excuses for not living up to them. Even in the schools—yes, at the precise points where the principles of conduct are brought to the fore— the disparity between professed principle and conventional working rules can be found. It must be there as long as the schools remain silent concerning the gap between adult standards and adult performance. If anyone doubts this, let him investigate any school, secular or religious, at the points where it touches upon morality in the sphere of either economics or industry or politics. He will find generalized ideals of thrift, honesty, work, fairness, sympathy, generosity, loyalty, law, patriotism, and the faithful use of the franchise. The pupil may form generalized standards for business, industry, and the state, but from the school he will not learn, except in the rarest instances, to what degree these standards already prevail, or where and how, if actually applied, they would be resisted. Further, the concrete meaning of various ideals is kept obscure because this meaning depends upon social facts that we do not like to talk about. We might take thrift as an example. What is thrift *as it is conventionally practiced?* It is, according to circumstances, the forced, pinching, never-ending anxiety of multitudes of workers who can hardly feed, clothe, and educate their children, or the systematic elimination of waste from the establishments of the 2 per cent of our population that owns 60 per cent of the property! Does the virtue of thrift mean making

one's self comfortable and contented in such a system, or does it mean squeezing into a favored place in the system (one of the 2 per cent if possible), or what? Similarly, what is the meaning of the ideal of hard work? Work for whom, and to what end? Does the ideal of hard work mean adapting one's self to the present industrial system?

These questions do not imply any fault-finding with the teaching of thrift and of hard work, but rather the necessity of noting the limitations of such teaching and particularly the concomitant learnings that go along with it. When we teach thrift and hard work do we inadvertently teach also the actually existing and everyday working notions of success, of business and industrial standards, and of the rightness of the system as a whole? When we teach love to men, do we teach also (inadvertently, of course), evasion of the law of love?

Similar questions are in order as to our teachings concerning our form of civil society. A government "of the people, by the people, and for the people"; a society in which barriers of birth are abolished, and sheer manhood counts; a land in which every child may receive an education at public expense; the homeland of freedom of thought, of speech, of press, and of assemblage; equality of rich and poor before the law; a refuge for the oppressed of all lands; a nation that does not covet its neighbor's territories; a humanitarian civilization at last—what does all this, which we teach to all the children, signify as education? Does it signify that pupils are being trained to base their actions as citizens upon these ideals, actually holding legislatures, courts, and administrative officers of government to these good old tests of government; or, does it signify, rather, emotional response to an imaginary America, without frank recognition of the difference between the imaginary and the real? If the latter, then this apparently idealistic moral teaching becomes, as a matter of fact, a mantle that covers faults that need to be exposed in order that they may be corrected. At the best the result is duality of codes—lip-loyalty to the ideals to which our history leads us, but subservience to contemporary forces that resist the ideal.

These are not exceptional difficulties, but samples of a universal problem for education, whether in state schools or in church schools. The very same process whereby moral law secures control of the young carries with it habituation to moral duality, the acceptance of standards but non-expectation of obedience to them. In other words, we are developing in the young two inconsistent codes, with all the self-sophistications that this involves. As matters now stand, one can be a good man, a good citizen, and a good churchman, and yet acquiesce, with one's social group, in institutional habits that contradict and defeat one's conscientiously held principles.

3. But a remedial principle, as we have seen, is available, not only in adult experience but in child experience as well. It is the direct facing of good and evil, and the free exercise of judgment upon them. Herein the dynamic of moral evolution as a whole resides. We teachers need to make clear to ourselves that we may get different and even inconsistent results in our own thinking on specific facts of human life according to the ethical category through which we make our approach. If, for example, we contemplate together a west-side privileged child and an east-side unprivileged one, we

can easily see that something or other that depends upon the purposes of men is not good enough, yet we may not discover in relation to the facts an instance of neglect of duty or of doing what is not right. Obviously we must revise our notions of right and duty in a case like this. It is through the progressively self-evidencing good that we increasingly discover what is the duty of man.

What sort of men, women, and children are we producing by our interactions with one another and by our failures to interact? This is the basic moral test. A factory or a mine produces something besides commodities; it modifies human life directly. A newspaper does not merely purvey news and opinion, it is not just a container by means of which something is conveyed to us; it is a mode of contact of men with men wherein levels of human life are being determined. Civil government is not just a mechanism that can be understood by reading the constitution; it is a complex of living, pulsating human forces that are making men what they are. But our conventional standards of right and duty do not test any one of these three by any direct inspection of the human welfare or ill-fare to which they contribute. And these three are typical.

Often and often we dodge this sort of test—this invitation to promote moral evolution—by doing humane acts in alleviation of the consequences of our system (which means the consequences of doing right and our duty according to the conventional understanding of them), and then patting ourselves on the back because we are so responsive to human need! Undoubtedly the most difficult job that any moral leader of adults has to undertake is to induce them to gaze steadily at the consequences of their conduct. "Mother, what is meat?" asked a very small child at dinner one day. This question, the mother says, banished meat from the family table for months. The point of this story is not that meat should be banished, but that our comforts are produced at costs from which we habitually turn away our eyes. "Put myself in his place? Nay, why should I? He is doubtless in a place that is adapted to him, though it would not be to me." "He and I alike are parts of a system that I did not invent; if I had not been wise in my day the system would have put me where he is now." "God made us different, unequal; that's why." Anything rather than a matter-of-fact facing of human conditions just as they are, and asking whether this is just what we want.

Because children, as was hinted a little way back, have fewer of these acquired inhibitions, education is the precise sphere in which we can most certainly and economically strike at our moral dualism and evasions. Let us, then, go on to ask:

III

What does this discussion indicate as to the method of moral education?

It is commonly assumed that the greatest difficulty besetting the child in his moral growth is his tendency, because of his native impulses, to vary from his fellows. But in fact what most retards moral strength is the child's penchant for conforming to the ways of his fellows, particularly the ways of adults! Not until this truth is seen and acted upon shall we make much progress in methods of moral education.

At present—to speak broadly—three sorts of method are in use which, for the sake of brevity, we may call the mystical, the ritualistic, and the pragmatic. The first leads the pupil, through contemplation of noble characters or of noble virtues, to identify himself with ideals. The second, through salutes to the flag, songs, reiteration of loyal sentiments, selections from history, and participation in celebrations, induces the pupil to identify himself with an existing institution. The third helps pupils to solve the immediate problems of living together in pupil groups, whether in class or school-room, on the playground, or on Scout "hikes." Now, though each of these probably contributes something good, leaves some permanent deposit, and should be retained in our programs, nowhere within them do we find an induction into the greater moral issues of the time; nowhere in them do we find conditions that promise much transfer of school morality to the larger society; nowhere in them is there any hint of the defects, and therefore the moral pitfalls, in the things to which pupils are led to commit themselves in admiration and loyalty. On the other hand, we find here a positive tendency, especially in the ritualistic method, to produce moral illusion, and to create loyalties that are bound to resist moral progress. There is nothing here that can reasonably be expected to prevent the pupils from being sucked into the vortex of our customary faults.

Loyalty, affectionate loyalty, to some existing social group or institution is, in very deed, the beginning of moral wisdom. Hence the peculiar place of the family in any general scheme of moral education. The experience of fellowship, of "belonging," whether in

church, school, community, nation, world-society, God's
Kingdom, or even a boys' gang or a girls' set, is by all
means to be cherished. Loyalty, however, may mean
any one of several different things. Granted that within
it is always a moral germ, as the fidelity to one another
of the members of an outlaw band; the very fact that
this moral germ can survive within social imperfections
of every grade makes necessary a critical attitude toward
every loyalty whatsoever. When teachers lack this
critical attitude, when they induce pupils to plump their
attachments, especially when institutional attachments
take the form of pleasurable but unthinking crowd
excitement, then moral education is always in danger of
becoming immoral by sanctifying our social faults.

"Yes," I think I hear someone saying, "we must at
some stage of moral education take up the great questions of social reconstruction. When pupils have reached
postgraduate university rank, or possibly in their senior
undergraduate year, they may well approach, with
great caution, these difficult problems." Some bold
spirits would put the age as low as the high school;
scarcely anybody would begin the process in the elementary grades. But behold the folly of this post-
ponement. Comparatively few of our citizens ever
reach even the high school as yet. Moreover, for reasons
that need to be studied, the actual working morals of
our institutional life are scarcely ever brought to the
attention of the vast majority of college and university
students. Even if every college and university in the
country were a-quiver with the spirit of moral progress,
what could they do to bring about actual reconstruction?
They would be shut up, as so many academic reformers

are now, to palliatives for our pains; they would not reach the causes of our diseases. Unless, perchance, they noticed that our present methods of moral education, through undiscriminating loyalties, transmit the rooted evils as well as the rooted excellences of our social order!

The experience of active discrimination should begin just where the experience of loyalty begins; it should be a part of this experience and should grow with it. No one is loyal enough—not even a child is loyal enough—who does not note the grounds for loyalty, the excellences that call for admiration, the good that is worthy of preservation even at cost to one's self. But no one can effectively note this who does not at the same time and in the same act pick it out from among items that contrast with it. When this discrimination is lacking, the loyalties that are developed in the elementary grades are essentially partisanships or crowd enjoyments. And the result tends to be a well-meaning citizenry whose very loyalty makes them the tools of leaders who have an interest in maintaining the present imperfections of our institutions.

The most affectionate loyalty is ever that which recognizes the defects in the object of its devotion. Blind loyalty is never quite loyal enough, because it cannot help its object to overcome its defects. Absolute obedience, if there could be such a thing, would ignore personal qualities on both sides, and would therefore be a-moral. In the first line of method in moral education, therefore, we must have provision for encouraging the moral discrimination that leads on to moral creativity.

The lack of this factor, and of growth in this direction, accounts, I think, for the deadly conventionality of the colleges—the professors and the students have already graduated from the sort of moral education that was provided in their schooling! There is nothing in it that carries one forward. Nothing in the moral sphere is being created in the colleges; if there were, there would be more excitement. When a hen lays an egg she cackles. When moral reconstruction is attempted, opposition appears, a struggle ensues, sacrifice becomes necessary, and now and then a martyrdom occurs. When the great gods appear the lesser gods scream in fright. Youth, surely, is a period in which we should see and hear such things happening. Woe to the land whose young men and young women display none of the pangs of moral creativity![1]

Postpone the full project method in moral education to the college or the high school? Leave imitation, emotional manipulation, and camouflaged external authority in control in the grade school? No! For such a policy robs society of prime resources for its own self-renewing. Unwittingly it perpetuates our moral illusions and evasions. Even in the primary grades the full project principle is required—if for no other reason, as an offset to out-of-school conventionalizing processes. And the full project principle cannot be employed in any hedged-off experience, whether the narrow experience of schoolroom or in a Scout troop. Wherever the moral experience of the child occurs, wherever ethical assump-

---

[1] When students get sufficiently excited over a social issue to throw eggs at one who is discussing it, there is ground for hope. In the scale of intelligence, such egg-throwing is one degree higher than indifference.

tions are being formed, there is the field in which moral issues or problems are to be found, there certain of the essential data are to be sought, there good and bad are to be directly faced and judged, there moral conventionality is to be resisted and supplanted by moral thinking. There is, perhaps, no better place for initiating such a process than in a group within which several children find it necessary to live together, but the process will not reach its goal until it stretches out into the larger society of which the child is likewise a member.

When the Washington Conference on the Limitation of Armaments was in session, a first-grade class, because of practically inevitable contacts, became aware of what was going on, and of the fact that older persons were sending petitions to officers of our government. Of their own initiative, the children got up a petition of their very own, and printed it in crayon, each one signing his name. It read: "Please stop fighting." The whole thing was so serious, so real, it grasped the actual situation so firmly, that the teacher and principal did not feel at liberty to withhold this document from the Secretary of State. Let us not treat such incidents as pretty pictures of childhood over which to gush; the question is, Do children, in cases like these, perceive moral realities, and has their attitude any proper part in determining events? The more one studies incidents like this, the more significance one finds in the idea that childhood rather than adulthood is the typical figure in the kingdom of the good. At last, it dawns upon one that many of the great issues of society—war, for example —can be grasped, in essence, by the very young. The great wrongs in the world are those that deprive men of the simple, basic necessities that even children can feel the importance of, such as food, health, and liberty. And the steps that we must take in order to correct these wrongs are just such steps as children have to take almost daily in their struggle to live with one another.

Do you fear to open to children these major issues in society lest our adult defects should produce disrespect for mankind? If so, you have less faith than I in the soundness of human nature. Intimate acquaintance with the primary experiences of men, the experiences out of which arise the great social issues, broadens and deepens one's sympathy with all classes of men, wrong-doers included.

A few hints may now be given as to types of policy and procedure for developing children's capacity for moral creativity:

1. *Self-government projects.*—Make them real in the sense explained in the last chapter, and then help the pupils to develop regular and stated methods for always knowing and appreciating the motives, feelings, points of view of all parties, offenders included. Good order is never a sufficient end; understanding, and fellowship based upon it—fellowship between majority and minority, and fellowship between offended and offender—must always be aimed at, and methods for attaining it must be developed.

2. *Philanthropic projects.*—Let them include a study, not only of how to relieve distress or bring happiness, but also of the causes of distress, and what men are doing or not doing to remove these causes. Let the pupils get the point of view of relief agencies, and likewise of the persons relieved.

3. *Civic projects.*—Acquaintance with civic institutions and processes should not stop with knowledge of, and admiration for, our social machinery, however wonderful or worthy of praise it may be. Social causation should be revealed as at work—for example, how men become criminals; who corrupt police depart-

ments, and why; how civic reforms have been accomplished; who really pays the taxes, and so on. Attention should always be given to dissatisfied elements in the population, and always, along with loyal admiration, there should develop a realization of the unsolved problems that fall to the oncoming citizen.

4. *Current-events projects.*—One of the most unfair things that a teacher can do is to use current events, warm with feeling, to close the mind of the pupil to issues instead of opening it. These issues offer a peculiarly fine opportunity to deepen pupils' moral appreciations by living imaginatively in the experience of contending groups and parties. What is back of the incident? What final interest dictates the policy of this or that individual or group? What human need ought to have a hearing? These questions are far more important than the usual one, Who is right?

5. *History projects, and biographical studies.*—Not to furnish examples for imitation, not to sweep the pupil into an unthinking emotion of patriotism, but to deepen his insight into the facts and issues of life—this is the main purpose of biography and of history. This means neither hero-worship nor iconoclasm. It means neither untrue idealization of the past, nor gloating over its defects. It means never feeding a prejudice, but also never failing to see the nobility in men, both friends and enemies. Hence, method should be directed to: (*a*) Definition of issues in both individual and group conduct. What had to be decided? (*b*) Understanding of motives, or seeing through the eyes of other men. (*c*) Seeing how causes actually work in human life, especially in social institutions. (*d*) Discovering the unsolved problems of society. How different this is from the so-called teaching of history that culminates in a conviction that the really great problems are already solved, and that what we now have to do is to keep in motion the machinery that we have inherited!

6. *Projects related to business and industry.*—The main focus of the interest should never be profits, or mere processes, or efficiency defined in terms of extra-human products, but the human beings concerned, and what happens to them. If we make persons central we shall certainly find the importance of everything that

touches their well-being, but if we focus upon the means of well-being, we may never reach the human problem at all. What men, women, and children are affected by this industry, or this branch of commerce? What joys and sorrows come to them through it? What do they think about it? Does anything need to be improved, and if so how are we related to this improvement? The result will be a residuum, not only of intelligence as to how to carry on business and industry, but also of live human problems, together with data upon them, and the urge of fellow-feeling with all parties concerned.

7. *Projects related to modes of living.*—I here repeat a suggestion in an earlier chapter, that projects should be directed in all frankness toward understanding and evaluating types of home life, current amusements, sports, current reading-matter, the cultural institutions in the community, sorts of success and failure, the school itself. The great failures of our individual and social life should have a place here alongside of the great successes, and both should be traced to their roots. The disguises whereby we adults endeavor to make tolerable what should not be tolerated should be torn aside. The realities within class distinctions should be made to stand out. But nowhere in these projects should there be any propaganda, that is, attempt to transfer conclusions without thinking, but rather material and stimulus for doing one's own thinking.

8. *Projects in world-friendship.*—Perhaps this phrase will explain itself, but lest it should not do so, I will point out the possibility of deliberately extending our acquaintance with our fellows with a view to contributing to the formation of a genuine world-brotherhood. Playing games with population elements that are usually separated from us geographically or socially; getting acquainted, by visitation or by correspondence, in such a way that mutual helpfulness is developed; even living imaginatively as neighbors with people on the other side of the world—this is still another mode of learning what life is, what its problems are, and to some extent how they can be solved. Projects of this type can be linked with study projects concerning the actual international situation, the relation of commerce and foreign invest-

ments thereto, and the inefficiencies of current statesmanship. Is it not clear that one essential step toward a warless world is to subject the pseudo-wisdom of the wise to the real wisdom of the simple-hearted?

Some possible doubts about such a project method in moral education must now be considered.

1. Will projects like these unduly burden the sympathies of children? Not unless teachers make the mistake of "working upon the feelings" of pupils, or introduce them without reason to gruesome sights. The policy should be steadily pursued of utilizing evil merely as a necessary background upon which to display the good in sharp outline.

2. Will such projects make cynics of the young? Not unless someone leads them in cynicism. If the teacher really believes in the past enough to see in it a prophecy of a better future, problems of reconstruction of life should cause the classroom to be pervaded by eager hope.

3. Will these projects make sentimentalists of the young because of the gap between aspiration for a better world and ability to do anything effective to bring it to pass? If two conditions are met, this will not occur. The two conditions are that scientific method be used in the discovery and demonstration of causes and effects, and that appropriate action, within the capacity of the pupils, be constantly taken with respect to conditions in school, home, community, church, state, nation, and foreign lands that the pupils are already able to influence. See chapter v.

4. Finally, will this policy make radicals of the young? If by being radical we mean readiness to make changes without stopping to think, no; for this is a method of producing deeper thinking, and more widely distributed thinking, than we have ever had. The method tends to produce reflective obedience at the precise point where thoughtless discontent might "break the china." . . . . If by being radical we mean insisting upon applying some social dogma without due regard for the consequences to others, again no; for the method is the direct opposite of the dogmatic. . . . . If by being radical we mean stiff adherence to a

class interest, still again, no; for this method—and as far as we know, this method alone—will develop sympathetic understanding of the experience of all classes. . . . . If by radical we mean holding one's self above moral law and the helpful authority of the past, decidedly no; for this is the only known method whereby what is worthy of respect can be disengaged from that to which respect is no longer due. The greatest obstacle to respect for authority is the company it keeps. . . . . But if by being radical we mean readiness to form ideals, and heartily to believe in applying ideals in practice; if we mean facing unflinchingly the actual human situation anywhere, and readiness to make changes in our individual and social life as fundamental as the needs that are perceived—changes in the interest, not of a class, but of men just as men—then, yes, this method will make radicals. And "this is the intention, sir!"

CHAPTER VIII

THE SCHOOL AND ECONOMIC LAW

The thought-directed energies of civilized man—his projects—are predominantly devoted to economic problems and activities. The adult male, with relatively few exceptions, daily expends his freshest hours upon making a living or accumulating property; the adult female, if she is not an employee of others, occupies herself with the immediate economies of the home. The uncertainties and the anxieties that arrest attention and make men think are concerned, most of all, with these occupations and the products thereof. Even in our "higher" or "more spiritual" enterprises—domestic, religious, humanitarian, artistic, scientific—the economic factor is practically omnipresent, and not seldom it is prominent.

Therefore, the present tendency to bring the schools into closer relations with our economic activities is fundamentally (though not necessarily in all its present details) in the interest of realism and life-likeness in the educative experience. School-experience is obviously the natural place for the initiation of the young into all the basic factors of the social life, the economic included. Accordingly, the discussion that is now to follow presupposes that the schools will depart farther and farther from the standards of leisure-class education, and will ultimately become saturated with economic consciousness. Against this saturation I not only do not protest;

I regard it, rather, as a necessary phase of the mastery of life-processes by thinking. But much—almost everything—depends, first, upon getting into the school consciousness the reality of the economic order, not illusions concerning it, and second, upon establishing and maintaining genuine continuity between school projects and the projects of industry and of business. It behooves us, then, to inquire:

I. How, as a matter of fact, children do now come under the control of economic forces and acquire economic consciousness.

II. Whether the conceptions thus acquired are true to fact, and whether the accompanying attitudes are morally justifiable.

III. Whether or not business and industry, as they are now constituted, carry forward the project experience as it is understood by educators, or check and thwart it. Is there fundamental harmony, or fundamental inconsistency, between project method and real life?

I

How, then, does the economic order become incorporated into our thinking and our purposing? To what extent do children get their introduction to it through systematic, well-considered school procedures, and to what extent through hit-and-miss extrascholastic experiences? To ask this question is to answer it. The young obtain their notions concerning economic laws and processes, and they form their economic attitudes, almost entirely through out-of-school contacts with business and industry, together with the social ramifications thereof. Such facts as the following come very early into the circle of children's experiences:

The dependence of satisfactions upon money.—I have asked several large groups of adults at what age children first come to realize this. The usual answer is, at five years or less. Probably most children begin to spend money before the age of six, and have a distinct liking for the possession of it.

The sources of the family income.—The father works at a trade, or practices a profession, or keeps a store, or what not, and the children are aware of the fact and of its relation to income.

The distinction between employing and being employed.— Though there be no family servants, the distinction is soon known and felt. Some member of one's own family is employed; the delivery boy is hired by the grocer; the conductor and the motorman on the trolley car work for somebody else. Then comes the labor strike, with the imitative taking of sides.

The fact of poverty.—"The poor ye have always with you," and they are always mentioned in one way or another. Scarcely anything else is a more obvious, stated, and expected fact of our economic order.

Social distinctions based upon income or upon possessions.— Differences in apparel or in playthings; differences in the size and surroundings of dwellings; between "shanks' horses" and milady's limousine; between the laborer's table and the glitter of fashionable hotels; the aloofness of certain children from others—these and many other common facts make a groove in the child's mind between social classes.

The economic conception of success, and the prestige of wealth.— Ideas of this sort are often instilled through fairy stories; they arrive early, anyhow, through the talk that the child hears. Such a one is worth millions, or he is making loads of money—spoken with admiration often approaching awe. Every child knows, even in tender years, that wealth means influence, being looked up to, social greatness.

Thus, before a child enters the school his notions of life are likely to have come under partial, but usually effective, control of the existing economic order. After he enters school, the same influences surround him in his out-of-school time; he participates more and more in buying, selling, earning, and employing; he hears, sees, reads about business or industrial events such as successes and failures, competition, speculation, labor disputes. Meantime, within the school his main occupations are studies and plays that have only incidental relation thereto. This incidental relation may sometimes have significance, but the main fact is that, while the school does only a little to form his economic ideas and attitudes, the economic system itself continually seeps into his thinking and his character.

What, then, are the notions and the attitudes formed thus through the pressure of environment? Obviously the very ideas and attitudes that prevail in the economic life itself, and in the ramifications of economic standards throughout society. The system assimilates the young to itself by what is called informal as against formal education. Continuously, pervasively, everywhere, with every child, the process goes on. Differences of emphasis and of point of view occur, according to the economic class with which a given child is associated, so that children of privilege and children of poverty see things somewhat differently. Yet, as a rule, the two see only complementary sides of one and the same thing, so that the opposite attitudes that develop are likewise complementary and truly representative of inner strains of the economic order itself. It is safe to assume that within the preadolescent (or at most, early adolescent) growth of nearly all children assumptions and attitudes like the following are formed:

That a good bargain or successful deal is one in which you get the most for yourself, with no necessary thought of what the other fellow gets.

That one's purpose in business or industry will be to get possession of property and control of men. Persons who have a thought beyond immediate maintenance—and in nearly all families there is such thought—aspire to possess enough to make themselves secure against the contingencies of life, and to get into, or remain within, the class of employers. That business and industry should exist for the sake of producing goods to supply the needs of men, and that the true test is service to one's fellows—no such idea is within the horizon of children simply because it is scarcely within the horizon of business and industry themselves.

That the standard of success is not merely what one gets by earning it, but also and more what one gets as profits. One aspires, therefore, to be lucky, shrewdly venturesome, a sharp bargainer, cunning,, rather than creative and productive.

That there is nothing disgraceful in carrying this grasping process as far as the law allows, though ideally one would somewhat further limit such conduct as deception, taking advantage of another's ignorance, or capitalizing another's helplessness (helplessness arising, say, from hunger or from having a family to support). The Great War gave a startling demonstration of the morals of business when many a man of means gladly gave a son to the country, and then turned around and took enormous profits from the same country simply because it was in trouble and he could take unusual advantage of it.

That this getting for one's self is a competitive process, which is a more or less refined grabbing or seizure, or using one's wits to get more than others, so that where one man gains other men lose or at least miss the mark. This notion is considerably modified in labor circles by an assumption, growing out of labor-union history, that laborers will restrict competition with one another.

That this competitive struggle naturally and justly leads one to ally one's self with the class that best serves one's self-interest, hence, capitalist with capitalist, employer with employer, laborer with laborer. This assumption, too, is modified in certain labor circles by aspiration to make all men workers and therefore members of one only class.

That a successful career means, for a boy, to get into some sort of privileged position, to get ahead of one's fellows ("getting on in the world" it is sometimes called), and for a girl, being able to spend at will.

That the harshness and self-seeking that all this involves will be moderated by gifts to charity or to one's church, and by at least some generosity or high-mindedness, especially between economic equals, or in one's club, but that these will be only fringes upon the garment.

Though children's thinking may not sharply define these concepts and attitudes, nevertheless the concrete meanings of them, the forces and man-ways indexed by them, are not only familiar to children, but also accepted as the reality, the to-be-expected-as-a-matter-of-course in human conduct, their own included.

The Sunday schools and the public schools endeavor to present contrary ideals of personal conduct—loving one's neighbor as one's self, for example. But these are rarely taken as principles for business and industry. What we are in this sphere speaks so loudly that children cannot hear what we say. As a matter of fact, how deeply do we ourselves mean what we say? Surely, to assume the legitimacy of the principles upon which we do business, and then to advise children to love one another as equals, is to cherish a basic inconsistency. No mental or moral wriggling will enable us or the children to serve both God and mammon. We really serve the master of our daily labor, whoever this master is. And children, realistic and unsophisticated, take our conduct rather than our professions, our unuttered assumptions rather than the words that we judge fit for young ears, as the clue to the real forces of the human world.

These economic forces and laws, operative under the eyes of everyone, yet not fully avowed, and never put into textbooks, constitute one of the most stupendous of all educative forces. Silently, unnoticed by the child or by his elders, the young mind bends into conformity to the system. It is taken for granted because it is omnipresent and practically unchallenged. Moreover, it seems to be a thing of nature, for indeed it appeals to native traits, such as getting, accumulating, holding, emulating, mastering, admiration for power, and fondness for being admired. It makes, likewise, another profound appeal—to our fears. To be sure to have enough, and to provide against contingencies for one's self and for one's children—such contingencies as unemployment, sickness, old age, low prices or high prices—all this seems as natural as seizing food when one is hungry.

Thus, in short, *the system as it is* impresses itself upon the young as both natural and right, as natural law and moral law combined. Later, when they become immersed in economic processes, the assumptions thus passively accepted in childhood become foundation stones for the "rationalizations" that are so characteristic of the adult economic intelligence, and we then hear of immutable economic principles, and of the sacredness of this golden calf that our own hands have fashioned.

II

Of course this hit-and-miss education sadly mixes error with truth, evil with good. The process, described in chapter vi, whereby the young take the customary as the right and proper, is in full force in the economic sphere as well as in the sphere that we conventionally recognize as ethical. Indeed, the two spheres overlap, or rather, the ethical includes the economic. For, if it is true, as I have asserted, that the thought-directed energies of civilized man are predominantly directed to economic problems and activities, and if, as is obvious, economic action involves relations between men, even highly organized relations, then the economic order is not only *a* region of moral experience and of moral law, it is the chief region thereof.

We teachers have been lacking in moral realism. We have said, or assumed, that the character of children is formed chiefly by family relationships, play, and school experience (whether in the public school or in the school of the church), whereas character is formed chiefly by contacts with "the work of the world." Wherever men's energies chiefly go, particularly their thought-directed energies, there are the issues that men feel most constantly, and thither the feeling of the young goes. If, then, it is the duty of the school to introduce the young to business and industry just as they are—and I hold that this is a duty of the school—we teachers must put them upon a higher plane than has been customary, and to this end we must sift out fact from error, the morally forward-looking from the morally backward-looking. We must give up both our misleading silences and our misleading idealizations. We must introduce the young to business and industry just as they are. Not just as they think they are, for the economic struggle is characterized by overreadiness for action (with the accompanying tendencies to self-deception described in chapter iii), whereas the school must represent reflection and questioning. Not just as they would like to be thought, for the school must penetrate beyond conventionalities to realities. Finally, not just as they are viewed by those who, having been wronged and embittered by the system, see only badness in the men who profit by it.

Well, then, granted that pupils should be made acquainted most literally with gainful occupations and processes, what errors of fact, and what dangers of moral foreshortening need to be guarded against? The answer to this question will furnish partial guidance to any teacher who has occasion to introduce projects that are related to making a living, thrift, supporting dependents, understanding the processes of production and distribution, the study of vocations, and grasping current events and issues in the world of business and industry. The following list is only a classification of suggestive material; it makes no pretense of gradation or sequence; yet in it will be found problems applicable to all grades.

A. *The school should expose the falsity of the cynical self-justification, "Everybody looks out for number one."* In the sense in which this is intended, it is not true. The motive of gain is not nearly the universal control of conduct, even in economic relations. As father and mother labor for their children, and as men and women support their aged parents, so the researcher, the artist, the poet, the religious prophet are moved by a more creative urge than mere self-interest. So, too, the welfare of others is consciously carried upon the conscience of teacher, physician, pharmacist, motorman, electrician, locomotive engineer, ship's pilot, telephone operator—indeed, where shall the list stop? Where will children want the list to stop?

B. *The school should bring into clear relief the socially constructive measures already in operation, especially experiments in the*

humanitarian and democratic reconstruction of human relations.
I say "bring into clear relief," meaning thereby, not that they
should be promoted through the schools, but used as necessary
data for understanding business and industry as they are, and for
making clear the sort of problems that the new generation must
face. The sharing of profits; the sharing of management; boards
of arbitration in industries; co-operative societies; labor legislation;
education of the workers; legal restraint of monopoly; the con-
servation of natural resources—here is a partial list of contemporary items to which the coming years will surely add. Closely
related to these are various approaches to economic and labor
problems by individuals and organizations. Every school child
should know about the work of the Child Labor Association, for
example, and likewise everyone should learn about the industrial
and economic principles avowed by Jewish, Catholic, and Protes-
tant bodies. These need not be used after the manner of propaganda at all, but as data upon the existing situation and the problems that it necessitates. An incidental effect will be a further
revelation of widespread idealism in a sphere that is often represented as merely sordid or at least selfish.

C. *The school should reveal the darker as well as the brighter
side of our economic life.* The point is not that the school should
mete out blame to any individual or class, but that it should be
unflinchingly realistic as to the life that the children are moving
toward. Why do we shrink from such realism? Is it because our
deeds are evil, and we wish to conceal them? Or is it simply that
we are ashamed and helpless? In either case, we need the help
of the children, help that can come only from those who grow up
in the habit of seeing facts as they are rather than through the
eyes of partisanship, and in the habit of thinking, and of thinking
together, upon the major concerns of society. Let me make as
explicit as possible that the whole theory of method for which this
essay stands forbids making the schools an agent of any sort of
partisanship; but the theory insists that facts as they are, without
partisan selection, be made accessible, and that the young become
practiced in thought-analysis with respect thereto.

D. *The school should expose the falsity of the doctrine that our
competitive economic order, with the domestic broils and the foreign*

wars that it breeds, is an unavoidable expression of unchanging human nature. It is natural, of course, perfectly natural under some conditions, to seize, hold on, and fight for possession or mastery. But it is natural also, perfectly natural, to enjoy seeing others eat and enjoy themselves, to enjoy the good opinion of others, and to co-operate with them. Which of these opposite possibilities of human nature shall prevail is a matter of training, which may be, in turn, a matter of deliberate choice. It is no more true that our innate selfishness makes this economic order than that this economic order, through the training process already described, makes us selfish. As far as human nature is concerned, there is nothing to forbid the hope of reconstructing our economic life so as to make it a co-operative brotherhood.

E. *The school should expose the irrationality of pure profits.* By pure profits I mean the surplus that is taken by capital after paying all the costs of production, in which I include not only raw material, wages of labor, and interest upon capital, but also wages of management, and insurance of risks to capital. This surplus, this "velvet," which is the goal of so much striving, cannot allege any justification for itself whatever. It is property taken simply because, by virtue of some privileged position, one can take it and prevent others from doing so. The hope for this surplus, this profit-motive, continually subordinates production and humanity, causes wastage and wreckage, and then disguises its true character by fallacious talk about human nature.

F. *The school should show why a system that makes profits its standard of efficiency and success necessarily works against the public interest.* It exploits natural resources for the benefit of this generation (rather, a small fraction of it). It wastes precious resources upon costly competition, as in socially useless advertising and competitive selling, and makes the public foot the bill. Because it is competitive, it tends, in the nature of the case, to treat labor as a commodity, to be purchased at the lowest possible price. Indeed, the profit-engine makes not only the laborers, but even the managers and owners, little more than cogs and wheels, because nowhere is the final test any human good for anybody. It seeks to increase its privileges by influencing legislation and the administration of law, so that much of our law, as a matter of fact, is not directed toward the general welfare at all, but toward the further aggregation of power on the part of those who already have too much. It seeks foreign markets, and then foreign investments for surplus capital, secures control of governments for the protection and advancement of its foreign interests, gets into conflict with foreign business, demands strong armies and navies for "national defense," and leads nations into war.

G. *The school should help dispel current confusions with respect to the nature and ethics of property.* Confusion in thinking invites partisanship and conflict, and the misuse of potential good. Now, it is fair to say that the public mind as a whole is confused as to the nature of property as determined by its history, and as to the ethics of the situations that continually confront us. In particular, fog, dense fog, surrounds the common phrase, "the sacredness of private property." The phrase seems not inherently inappropriate, for surely there is a sense in which food is sacred, likewise the family roof, the tool with which one creates either commodities or beauty, the earth whence all our sustenance is derived. Not until something of sacredness attaches to these things shall we rescue them from bad uses. But are all types of private property through all history sacred, or only some? Property is a changing right, being redefined or modified from time to time, our own time included. Again, to whom is private property sacred, and wherein lies the meaning of this sacredness? Is it sacred to God? If so, what is his will with regard to the distribution and the use of it? Is it sacred to some human ideal? If so, what ideal, and how can possessions be made to promote this ideal? Or, is it sacred to the arbitrary desires of its possessor? How would such sacredness differ from pure profanity? Or do we mean that sacredness attaches to all or some American laws or traditions as to property rights? Is there not room for just a suspicion that some particular law or privilege is seeking to perpetuate its merely temporary self by falsely identifying itself with an eternal principle whereby all forms of property are to be judged? The least that the school can do is to point out these three simple, non-partisan principles: (a) The sacredness of life itself attaches to the things that make life and growth and happiness possible. (b) The right of property has a long evolution; it has passed through different forms and stages; it is still evolving, and is susceptible of improvement. (*c*) The sacredness of property at any stage of its evolution can be made credible only by showing that it really ministers to the good life on the largest possible scale.

H. *Whenever the community is divided the school should help its pupils to understand all parties.* This means both majorities and minorities. We are developing in this country antagonisms that are dangerous and destructive. We theoretically deny that there is any sound basis for class divisions, yet we are producing class divisions and intensifying them at a fearful rate. One of the ways in which we do it is this: We give to the young conclusions instead of data concerning classes, parties, and movements. We do this in the homes, in conversation, in the public prints, and even in the schools. The result is that we do not even want to get acquainted with certain of our fellow-citizens, and we do not really understand them. We thus close the one possible road to social health, which is thinking together upon common problems. There is pressing need that the schools should develop a primarily humane and neighborly attitude toward the members of every faction, toward the maligned capitalist and toward the maligned I.W.W. or other discontented person. One might plead this on the ground of good sportsmanship or clean fighting. But higher ground can be alleged; it is that, having committed ourselves to the principle of managing our general interests through the general will, we have therein committed ourselves to thinking by the people themselves as the mode of control; that, to start this popular thought going, and then withhold in our educational system the data for thought, and even prevent the relations between citizens that can alone make common thinking possible, is the sheerest folly from every point of view. It is the way to make dense radicals and dense conservatives alike, and ultimately to substitute explosion for regulation by thought. No, the schools must help us to get acquainted with one another, so that we shall find out how human we all are, and at last discover what it is that is hurting us all and robbing us of the friendship that belongs to us.

The main outcomes of such a policy in the schools would be as follows: First, vocational preparation for business and industry, even as they are at present organized, would be furthered.   Second, citizens of all classes —capitalists, managers, and workers—would begin their career knowing what are the major problems of their generation.   What could be more disjointed than an educational system that sends forth young people unconscious of the social problems that need to be solved, and bent only upon enforcing some trouble-making conventional point of view?   Conversely, who can estimate the acceleration of social progress that would result if the schools should only get the hang of teaching how to find the major problems, how to find data upon them, and how to think together?   Third, the young would begin their economic careers with a more realistic set of assumptions, with clearer insight into moral situations, and with ambitions better related to the welfare, the peace, and the progress of society.

III

But would not this educational policy unfit the young for our economic order?   Would not the contrast between the school and after-life be too great?   Let us squarely face this doubt.

In the project principle as it is now developing there are three aspects that are of first importance for our present problem: (a) Purposeful activities of the pupil himself are believed to constitute the most educative sort of experience, and purpose is conceived to include thinking—on occasion, the whole gamut of it, from feeling a problem and defining it, on through the forming of hypotheses and the gathering of data, to experimental and other methods of testing. (b) The pupils are led to discover problems not merely in subject-matter and school conditions that are prearranged by school authorities, but also, and perhaps preferably, in "life-situations" that arise spontaneously, school or no school. (c) An especial point is made of leading pupils to do all this discovering, thinking, purposing, planning, executing, and criticizing *together*. At no other point is the contrast between the "old pedagogy" and the project principle quite as sharp, I believe, as it is here. Instead of asking whether the pupil sees and agrees with the teacher, we are more concerned that pupils should see and agree with one another, each helping the other to be objective-minded, and all together arriving at common knowledge and common purposes, or else at differences that all can understand and respect.

How does this sort of experience compare with real life in the economic sphere? The answer is, or ought to be, startling. In the vast majority of the operations of the vast majority of men one rarely finds or solves a problem, one does not think (for this is not what one is paid for doing), much less is there any thinking together. One rarely forms or executes purposes of one's own except the one monotonous purpose to finish one's task and draw one's pay. Creating a product that expresses one's self—this belongs to the privileged few. Thinking together, and creating together—this is done in advance in the inner offices of the establishment. Even the owners of the capital, the scattered stockholders, rarely do any thinking or planning with respect to production. They merely draw the dividends or pocket the losses that have been brought to pass by managers who may be hundreds of miles away. As to common enjoyments, who goes to a factory or a department store, or a counting-room for any such purpose? No, one flies from one's occupation in order to find freedom, joy, and fellowship.

Even where, as in managerial circles, thinking and creating are experienced, the "togetherness" is limited and ungenerous, for a part of the purpose is to concentrate benefits in the few by getting ahead of competitors. And the sphere of one's creativeness is restricted. Some of the zest of inquiry, discovery, productivity, is here, to be sure, but not enough to fill men's capacities. For managers are bound by a rigid business orthodoxy that forbids large social experimentation. As in a vise, the standard of profits holds their thinking. If they yield to some humanitarian motive, they feel themselves under obligation to prove that it is profitable. Imagine the slavery of the mind in a system that requires one to camouflage one's most manly acts! Consider the limitations of men who are not allowed to plan any better way of feeding the world than by competition in food-stuffs! We have seen eminent men spending themselves and their substance generously in charity drives to feed starving multitudes but at the same time insisting that prices should be fixed by competition.

There results a deplorable lack of individuality, a dull monotony of the type "business man." And there results, likewise, lack of foresight. Consider, for example, the way in which large employers have commonly resisted legislation directed to the safety and welfare of employees—bills that require factory owners to place safeguards around dangerous machinery are an instance. Of course, the general effect of such laws is to make the consumer pay for the safety of the employee. All that was necessary, then, even from the employer's point of view, was to induce employers in different competing states to push everywhere for the enactment of such laws. But such thinking together, even with other manufacturers, is not characteristic, and so legislation of this type was opposed even when anyone with half an eye could see that it would inevitably pass. The point of this illustration is, not that manufacturers are different from other persons, but that the present presuppositions of business so cramp human powers that men even of great ability are almost automatically made into reactionaries.

It is true that economic life, is on the whole, a system of control by thinking. To this extent it is project experience. But how undeveloped in the case of both employer and employee, and how inferior to our better schools in freedom, freshness, objectivity, and co-operation. Clearly, schools that employ the project principle with anything like thoroughness cannot prepare the young for continuing unchanged our present modes of economic life. And who can desire that this should be done? It would amount to maintaining sick schools in order to perpetuate a sick society. Our problem is to maintain healthy schools to the end that society may healthily change and grow. The basis upon which alone this is possible is the one already so fully indicated: Let the school stick to whatever is known to be true either scientifically or historically, and let it cultivate in each new generation that which is at once the most conservative and the most radical thing in life, sincere respect for all men. On this basis we might maintain healthy schools even in a sick society.

CHAPTER IX

THE HEALTHY SCHOOL IN A SICK SOCIETY

It may be assumed-- probably no one would contest the assumption—that schooling is intended to represent and prepare for society, not just as it is, but as it would like to be, or at least as it is capable of becoming. We do not say to pupils: "Use the English language as the majority use it"; or, "Govern your city as majorities always have governed it"; or, "Manage international affairs by good, old-fashioned diplomacy"; or, "Maintain the competitive system just as you find it"; or, "Take sides in the class struggle just as we are doing"; or, "If your morality is as high as ours, it is high enough"; or, "You need not be any more humane than we are": no, we select the men, the incidents, the phases of life to which to expose the young, and we hide from them much of what we are, hoping that they will escape some of the pits into which we have fallen.

Such being our habit—such being the nature of schools—it should cause no surprise or embarrassment that almost throughout the preceding chapters education through rationally purposeful activities of children has appeared to be antithetical to common ways of adults. In any progressive civilization, surely, the school should be expected to be ahead of society, and therefore to embody a critique upon current modes of life. Whoever presents the purposes and methods of education—whether the project principle or any other—in such a way that no strain is felt between them and our adult ways, does thereby convict himself of misrepresenting the educative process. He misrepresents, in fact, his own age, which does not desire merely to be copied by the next generation. We are sodden enough, but not so sodden as not to want others to be better than ourselves. Here, in this self-criticism, this divine discontent, latent and confused though it be at times, is a chief glory of human nature. Ours is a self-reconstructing nature. If it puts its ideals at times into cold storage, it at least does not destroy them, and anon it brings them forth, applies them, and reconstructs them. The contrast between school projects and adult projects that have cropped up all along our journey may, then, conceivably be a part of the evidence that we are on the right track. At any rate, we shall do well to see whither our discussion is going.

These, then, are the main antitheses between current adult life and the particular conception of school projects that this essay has endeavored to unfold:

Current adult life takes natural law inconsiderately as an invitation to exploit natural resources wastefully and selfishly, and to indulge worthless, self-defeating, injurious, or too costly desires. The school can help in this matter by developing projects that illuminate these facts, and oppose the wastes and burdens that otherwise will be entailed upon the next generation.

Mankind is by nature overready for action, and underready for objective self-judgment. Even the wisdom of our wisest leaders is therefore infected with a constant tendency toward irrationality. The school can help by developing in pupils a habit of self-criticism, and a corresponding habit of caution with respect to the projects of adults.

Our society exposes children and young people to a multitude of stimuli that tend toward overexcitement, fragmentariness, shallowness, and irreverence. The school can help by developing projects that sift the wheat from the chaff in these stimuli.

Our school laws are defective in that pupils, because they have no right to participate in school government, are not permitted to have any thoroughgoing experience of democracy. Further, our constitutions, unconscious of the principle of learning to govern by governing, grant the franchise upon the basis of mere age. The schools can take the initiative toward securing improvement in these laws and constitutions.

The moral life of men tends continually to become conventional and lacking in creative vigor. The reason for this is partly self-imitation and imitation of the past; partly that we maintain, alongside of our professed principles, a working, self-excusing code; partly that we let minor loyalties—our very virtues—blind us to the need of larger ones. The schools can help by developing discriminating loyalties, as against undiscriminating emotional ones; by cultivating moral realism in the form of direct, original judgments upon good and evil; and by practice in devising and revising standards in accordance with known needs of men.

The economic life of our time provides no sufficient experience of initiative and creativity, or of control by thinking, and especially by thinking together. Business and industry tend to become mechanized and inhuman. The privileged as well as the un-privileged are living cramped lives. The schools, by pursuing the project method in the direction of the economic order, can send into it young persons already habituated to thinking together, and already alive to the major problems that the new generation must face.

Problems and difficulties more or less like these will always confront the schools. They are normal to education as such. Yet we of the United States have reason to feel them with peculiar poignancy at the present moment. For the channels of progress that are normal to our experiment as a free people are seriously clogged. We believe ourselves to be highly progressive, yet we are fumbling the instruments of progress with half-palsied hands.   A deep distrust of reason has seized upon us, and we are sick and staggering and ill-natured as a consequence.   That this should occur in an age of unparalleled scientific and historical knowledge, and of unparalleled technic of many kinds, may appear to be paradoxical, but perhaps it is a part of our sickness that we confuse reason with the possession of a stock of facts, or handiness in amassing more facts, or ability to command great natural and human forces.   That we do deeply distrust reason is shown by the following characteristic tendencies of our society:

The prevalent distrust of mankind, and the accompanying belief in force—distrust of other peoples, with consequent reliance upon arms for security; distrust of immigrants, and insistence that they become like us or get out; distrust of the humanity in our economic opponents, and resort, in times of acute strain, to force of many sorts, including espionage, private hired armies, and partisan control of the agencies of government (administrative officers, police, even courts); distrust of the ability of government to govern, and resort to various organizations, some of them secret, that by lawless means endeavor to "make law and order prevail"; distrust of schools and of school teachers, and resulting legislation that calls for oaths of allegiance and "smelling committees"; distrust, even, of one's capacity for disinterested or noble conduct, and degraded acceptance of the doctrine that others must force us to be good or we shall not be good at all.

The growth of class consciousness, with its assumption that my class must prevail and others must go under.   This implies a denial that common ground exists that might be discovered by thinking together.   In effect it enthrones some special interest, some arbitrary and non-rational preference.

The revival of dogmatism in many directions, and the consequent growth of intolerance.   The widespread reactionism in religious thought is paralleled by a new, dogmatic, intolerant "Americanism," and by economic dogmatism that labels dissenters by terms intended to convey opprobrium, employs spies in order to entrap liberal professors and ministers and thus secure their removal from office, and finally induces the state to imprison the most helpless of the industrial dissenters.

Overgrown reliance upon institutional mechanisms, and loss of appreciation for informal association of men with one another. Almost everywhere we witness an enormous increase in the "overhead" part of organizations. As the "overhead" charges upon industrial production have almost reached the breaking-point, so the managerial functions in churches, colleges, school systems, and many kinds of associations, have come to be almost identified with the functions of these institutions and organizations themselves. The most sought-for man as administrator is the one who can keep masses of men contentedly moving in predetermined grooves. In short, it is assumed that men are to be manipulated, not stimulated to think. The many are taken to be, not so many minds that might shine of their own light, not possible creators and guides of a common rational life, but fingers, hands, tools, for those who arrogate wisdom to themselves.

The prevalent assumption that the things of the spirit can get on only by the favor of those who have great possessions. That men of means so generally believe themselves competent, by virtue of their business experience, to guide the destinies of colleges and universities, churches, and all manner of institutions, is not as much their own fault as it is a symptom of the general sickness of the age. The consequence is that living reason, which must produce out of its treasure things new as well as old, does not find itself comfortable in our institutions. How can it be, when it sees learning's own stamp, and religion's own stamp, with studied deference, placed upon mere ownership? An ominous hush prevails at just the points where learning should pass over into reason and wisdom, free criticism of institutions, and sacrificial labor for reconstruction. We have specialists in this and that field of research, and we have technicians who can tell us how to get whatever money or force can procure, but we grievously lack men who can and will tell us what sort of life, what sort of men, and what sort of social institutions are worth while, and how they can be produced.

The present rejuvenescence of the old Americanesque fear of our own freedom. Not content with a constitutional system that not only prevents hasty change but even makes it difficult to ascertain and record a changed will at all, we hedge ourselves about with unnecessary precautions against "going too fast" or "going too far." We have become more afraid of going too far than of not going at all, or of going in the wrong direction. One might suppose that reason, if given an open road, would sufficiently shun the unreasonable, and that the necessary caution for us inveterate imitators would be to be rational rather than slow, and to go far enough to satisfy the issues that are or ought to be before us. But no; having won our freedom, having established our right to think, to make changes, to follow reason, we turn about and only timidly and half-heartedly use the very privilege for which we should stake life itself.

The enormous increase (made possible to a large extent by advances in psychology) in effective schemes for doing the people's thinking for them under the pretense of giving them information and inviting them to judge for themselves. This is coming to be designated as propaganda. The essence of it is "getting over" your own predetermined view under some sort of false pretense. The shamelessness with which this art is practiced both by governments and by economic interests is amazing; and it is portentous, for most of the agencies of public information already have become engines of propaganda. When one reads the "news" dispatches in the respectable as well as the "yellow" press, one may be and often is subjecting one's self to subtle influences deliberately directed toward the formation of a particular opinion that may or may not be true, a self-commitment that may or may not be just. Thus, more and more, the human mind is assumed to be a thing to be manipulated, and persons, instead of being objects of infinite value, become commodities to be bought at auction.

Yes, our society is sick because it fears reason. What, then, do I mean by reason? Obviously not a body of already formulated propositions, but the thing in us that does the formulating, the criticizing, and the reformulating. The scientific attitude is a part of it, and this attitude is nowhere more in evidence than in the fact that the sciences continually grow by revising themselves. But other human wants also belong to reason, not only desire for knowledge, but also desire for beauty, desire for fellowship, desire for food and for whatsoever else makes knowledge, beauty, and fellowship possible. Wants, like science, have no fixed and irrevocable formulas. Often they emerge out of dimness into clear light; or they grow from seeds to great trees; and always misapprehensions of them may need to be corrected, and errors, even on a large scale, may have to be overthrown. But wants, thus co-ordinated, self-corrected, and growing, are inherent in rationality itself. Wheresoever desires and satisfactions are discriminated from one another, and thought is taken for supplying the approved want, there resides at least a germ of reason, which I, if I am to be rational, must recognize as there. In other words, mutual recognition or valuing of persons just as persons, mutual modification of one's own desires by valuing the desires of others, and co-operative thinking, purposing, and executing in the interest of what is mutually wanted—this is the very base line of rationality.

Now, this, precisely this, is the substratum of the project principle as it is developing in educational thought. The principle certainly outruns the ways of adult society, whether political, economic, ecclesiastical, or broadly cultural; yes, this principle will always outrun actual society because it is itself the principle of social growth. Now, *this outrunning of the ways of adult society is one of the essential functions of the school.* People want the school to do it, and they furnish the backing for doing it. Clumsy and unpractical as we Americans have been in handling our school problems, nevertheless there is truth in the old comment that the one common faith of all Americans is faith in education. The glad hope of a new, more humane civilization in this new land, so free from precedents, focused itself unerringly in the school as a chief organ of the better future. Indeed, how could one better describe the healthy school than as one in which society seeks the whole of the rationality that as yet it has only partly achieved? The healthy school expresses society's better self, by implication accusing its lower self, and by overt action revaluing its values, and above all affirming and practicing the social unity that is of the essence of goodness and of reason.

We can have healthy schools even in a sick society, just as we can have real science among men who are liable to fallacies and prejudices, and just as we can have public sanitation even when it runs counter to great financial interests. The key to health in our schools is knowledge on the part of educators of what social health is, and a right professional spirit. By "professional spirit" I do not mean anything that discriminates the salaried expert from wage-earning employees. Let us start, rather, from the other end, thinking of ourselves as servants, bound to do the will of our master. Who, then, is the master of the schoolmaster? Surely, not the board that votes our wages, for its members are fellow-servants with us, administrators, with us, of a public trust. Thus, our question goes back to this: Who is the master, who is to be served, when citizens, acting either as voters of the state, or as members of a

church, or even as private donors, determine that
schools shall be? Are they serving themselves? Obviously not in any large measure. Are they acting, then,
as servants of the children? Yes, and no; not the present narrow will of the children, but a hoped-for, rational
will. The master of the schoolmaster is the better,
or rational, self of society, whose property it is always
to judge actual society and always to point the way of
improvement. The superintendent, principal, teacher,
or college president who makes himself servant of pupils,
or of parents, or of boards of trustees, in any other sense
than this lacks the professional spirit and is in danger
of becoming pander rather than educator.

As the researcher in science or history serves neither
self nor party, but the truth; as the true physician, when
he faces disease, is guided neither by self-interest nor
by opinions of the patient nor by popular conceptions of
healing; as the faithful minister of religion endeavors to
obey God rather than men, so the real educator, enduring
(if need be) as seeing the invisible, leads forward into
freedom a society that is fettered by selfishness and by
institutionalized timidities. He leads society into freedom by leading children into it, and this he does by giving
them practice in it. He lets free that within us that is
ready to rebuke our selfishness, our partisanship, our
institutionalism and dogmatism, our aloofness and class-
feeling, and the nationalism that stands in the way of the
unification of mankind. This means, not freedom from
law, but freedom through law and through the making
of law. We grow free only as we extend and deepen the
bonds that unify us—only as we think, plan, act, judge,
and enjoy together.

INDEX

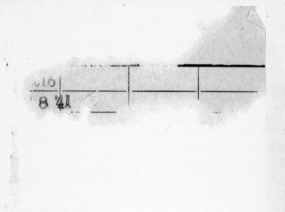

.016
8 41